THE SEVEN DEADLY VIRTUES

THE SEVEN DEADLY VIRTUES

Gerald Mann

WORD BOOKS
PUBLISHER
WACO, TEXAS

First Printing, May 1979
Second Printing, August 1979

ISBN 0–8499–2853–2
Library of Congress catalog card number: 78–65809
Printed in the United States of America

Quotations marked TEV are from the Today's English Version of
the Bible, copyright © American Bible Society 1976. Used by
permission. The quotation from *The Living Bible, Paraphrased*
(Wheaton: Tyndale House, 1971) is used by permission.

This book is dedicated to

POP BARROW

A man . . . but a man like God

CONTENTS

Introduction

THERE WAS AN Indian preacher out in New Mexico whose
congregation was so scattered that he had to deliver his weekly
sermons via smoke signals. It so happened that he was ex-
pounding the Gospel on the day the first atomic bomb was
detonated. The earth shook; he heard the distant rumble; he
saw the gigantic, mushrooming cloud. He looked down at his
meager fire. He looked up at the immense cloud. Then he said
wistfully, "Now *that's* what I've been trying to say!"

Such was my reaction when I happened upon the essay by
Dorothy Sayers that spawned the title of this book. The essay
is entitled "The Dogma is the Drama." [1] Miss Sayers has always been one of my favorite Christian apologists. She had the
eclectic mind and saucy wit to communicate a faith that made
sense during a period when the Church was under fire from
the arts.

Sayers believed that the assault on the Church was largely
the Church's own fault in that it had failed to articulate the
Christian message in categories that modern man could grasp
and apply. The Church had lost its imagination, as she saw
it. Instead of using its creativity, it had continued to crank out
hackneyed, sixteenth-century renditions of the same old song.

"We have efficiently pared the claws of the Lion of Judah," said Miss Sayers, "certified him 'meek and mild,' and recommended him as a fitting household pet for pale curates and pious old ladies." [2]

As a result of the Church's failure to be relevant to society, Miss Sayers felt that modern novelists and playwrights despised Christianity without even knowing what it was. They were not attacking the Christian gospel, they were attacking its acculturated shell.

To illustrate her point, Sayers poses a hypothetical interview in which an anti-Christian is being asked to define the beliefs of the Christian religion. At one point, the interviewer asks: "What are the seven Christian virtues?" The anti-Christian answers: "Respectability; childishness; mental timidity; dullness; sentimentality; censoriousness; and depression of spirits." [3]

Sayers then says: "Whenever an average Christian is represented in a novel or a play, he is pretty sure to be shown practicing one or all of the Seven Deadly Virtues enumerated above." [4]

"The Seven Deadly Virtues"—when I read those words, like the Indian, I wanted to shout, *"That's* what I've been trying to say!"

For a long time I have believed that what many Christians regard as virtues are in fact *deadly* virtues. They are deadly because they produce the precise opposite of their intentions. They are deadly because they serve as repellants, not magnets that draw persons to Christ. And most of all, they are deadly because they usually derive from a sincere desire to please God. Rarely have I encountered the kind of consciously pious hypocrite whom we often see portrayed in sermons, movies, books, and other forms of communication. In my opinion, most people who aspire to virtuous living, even if they are offensive, are sincerely attempting to do God's will.

Therefore, let me say at the outset that this work is intended to expose the unconscious hypocrisies that creep into our lives, not the conscious Pharisaisms that have been given so much play over the years. The dominant theme of this book is that *evil attacks the Christian, not at his weak points, but at his strong.* The deadliest sins are those that are born out of noble motives. The counterfeit currency that does the greatest harm is the kind that most closely resembles the real thing. So it is with Christian virtues. The deadliest are those that most nearly resemble true Christian virtues.

Perhaps another way to express the spirit of this book is to note that the sins of the noble-minded have worked more evil in the world than all of the deliberate vices put together. It was noble-minded, virtuous people who killed Jesus. Noble minds engineered the Inquisition. The landscape of history is littered with the gore and slaughter of noble-minded men who thought themselves to be bearing the banner of Christian virtue.

The most potentially dangerous man is the righteous man; because the more righteous he is, the more he will be tempted to think his deeds are divinely inspired. If he can be convinced that his deeds are motivated by God, he can be made to do almost anything.

Reinhold Niebuhr was thinking of the danger that stalks the pious, when he said: "Cursed be he that trusteth in man, even if he be pious man or perhaps, *particularly,* if he be pious man." [5]

Hence the convictions that lie behind *The Seven Deadly Virtues.* Although Miss Sayers has given me a form for expression, the substance of the pages that follow has come from my own personal pilgrimage as a Christian minister.

Long before I knew the names of those mentioned above, I began to experience how deadly sincere but misguided Christian piety can be. I was not reared in a home where formal religion was practiced, although my parents instilled in me many values I later discovered to be Christian. My earliest impressions of God were positive and friendly. My father's motto for living was: "Be honest; be forgiving; and never give up."

He was an uneducated child of poverty. By the time he reached forty, he had made a fortune, purchased a ranch in the country, and moved us there to live near a small town in Texas. It was there that I formally encountered Bible Belt religion, personified in the local Baptist congregation.

I loved the Baptists immediately. They were a jovial lot with obvious opinions. One needn't wonder where they stood on an issue; they'd tell you "right off," as they put it. Nor did it take them long to evaluate one's spiritual condition. The first time I met a Baptist preacher, he asked me about three questions, placed his hand on my shoulder, and said, "Jerry, you're lost, and that's all they are to that!"

I started attending church regularly. I didn't know what "lost" meant, but he said it with such gravity that I was certain I was whatever he said I was.

By the spring of my thirteenth year, the Baptists were "hard in prayer for my soul," as they frequently informed me. An evangelist was coming to town to lead revival services, and according to them, it could well be my last chance to be saved. Such ominous warnings didn't frighten me. What little I had had to do with God told me that he was not that kind at all.

However, I attended the revival anyway, because the evangelist was a former teen-age gang-leader who had once tried to stab my older brother. I was curious to hear and see a person who claimed to have been converted from the seamy side of life.

The ex-hoodlum-turned-Bible-thumper was something to behold! He was dressed in white and red—white suit with red cuffs and lapels, red and white shoes. Even his Bible was red and white!

His sermon was a blow-by-blow account of his former life on the "wild side." Graphically, he portrayed scenes of gang fights, heroin sales, and sexual liaisons with wanton sirens.

Considering that the wildest thing in our town was playing dominoes at the pool parlor, one can imagine how captivated we teenagers were. This was genuine Mickey Spillane stuff! And in the flesh! We didn't miss a word.

Then he told us of how Jesus had reached into the midst of all that muck and plucked him out of it. I am certain he didn't intend to, but he made it sound as if Jesus had spoiled a rather exciting life! His message had the import of one of those *True Confession* magazine stories: "I immersed myself in a world of booze and dope and sex. And boy, was it fun! But I tell you my story only to keep you from making the same fun-filled mistakes."

The story was so gripping that I was sorry he had been converted so soon. I wanted to hear a little more! I had the same feeling as when I saw one of those Cecil B. DeMille Bible-movies. I liked Victor Mature better with his Roman uniform and beautiful girls than with his old robe and a plain Jane!

Anyway, after describing his conversion, the evangelist began his appeal to sinners (which included any and all of us who thought his former life was glamorous). The choir sang for a while and several people went forward.

Then the evangelist took the microphone and started down the aisle, while the songleader fed out the cord. In a flash, I realized he was heading straight for me. (Later, I learned that someone had "fingered" me as a potential convert.)

He stopped in front of me and said in a booming voice, "Do you want to go to Hell!" The audience was silent. I didn't know what to do. I was scared and angry and confused. I bolted from the pew, dashed outside, and ran two blocks before I looked back.

I relate this story for several reasons. For one thing, I vowed that day at the age of thirteen never to enter a church again, and I spent several years attacking the Church at every turn. My bitterness led me to flaunt every act which would anger the pious. I saw all Christians as hypocrites, or at best, as deluded, superstitious cripples. It would be several years before I would come to see that for all his gaudiness, that evangelist sincerely believed himself to be (and, *was,* in his own way) God's ally. In a word, this story shows how deadly a well-intentioned religious zeal can be. Again, the pious person is the one who stands in the greatest jeopardy of driving people away from the very God he is trying to proclaim.

The second reason I tell this story is because it has served as a constant reminder of what causes true Christian virtue to become deadly virtue. Essentially two things cause Christian virtues to become deadly virtues: guilt and pride. These two words will recur in the chapters that follow; however, let me relate them briefly to my experience with the evangelist.

The evangelist was dominated by a guilt-ridden religion. He no doubt carried a tremendous load of guilt because of his former life. He was trying to exonerate himself and to gain God's acceptance by using his former sins to call people to God. Instead of accentuating the new life he had found in Christ, he focused upon his former life of sin. Why? I believe it was because he thought his present life was unacceptable. Little did he know that he was already forgiven. If he had, he would have talked about that instead of giving a clinical description of his former life.

Guilt made him blot out the story of his new life. Pride did, too. I suspect that he felt the only way he could prove that he had truly changed from "bad" to "good" was by proving to others that they were "bad." No matter that he had to resort to cheap theatrical tactics.

Christian virtue is subverted to deadly virtue by guilt and pride. You will hear this again.

Finally, I relate the story because it has become something of a catalyst in determining my particular style as minister for the past twenty years. At age twenty, I encountered God in Jesus Christ at the same church from which I had bolted seven years before. There I met and courted my wife; there I was baptized; there I committed my life to preach the gospel; and there I received love and support from the same people whom I had formerly despised.

What happened to me in the spring of my thirteenth year was evil, but God turned it into good in his own mysterious way. The experience has served as a catalyst because it has taught me two things.

First, the Church, in spite of all of its spiritual warts and pimples, is God's Church, and he will accomplish his purpose through it. The people of the Church—most of them anyway —are God's people; but they are people nonetheless. That initial negative experience has reminded me over and over that God's people are still sinners. A minister must realize this and learn to be forgiving if he is to be of any use to them or God. There is no way for a minister to keep his spiritual and emotional balance unless he can forgive people, *including himself*, for being people. Most of the ministers I have known who have dropped out in disillusionment have made the mistake of expecting too much of themselves and of their people. In a word, the Church is not God, but it's God's!

Secondly, the "evangelist episode" taught me to be suspicious of all Christian piety . . . to be fearful of it . . . to examine it constantly . . . and, yes, even to punch holes in it at times. There is no such thing as the perfect piety. The person who thinks himself pious had better "watch out." As Pascal said: "There are only two kinds of men: the righteous, who believe themselves sinners; the rest, sinners, who believe themselves righteous." [6]

For centuries the Church has spoken of the Christian life within the context of the Seven Deadly Sins and the Four Cardinal Virtues. This book is about a third category, *The Seven Deadly Virtues*. Had it not been for a negative experience in the life of a thirteen-year-old child some twenty-six years ago, this book could not have been written. I will leave it to you to decide whether that negative has indeed proved to be a positive.

Each of the following chapters will deal with one of the virtues I call "deadly." I have borrowed two of the seven from Miss Sayers's list—I do not know if my treatment of them is what she had in mind, for, to my knowledge, she never defined them herself. They, along with five others, are the deadly virtues that seem to me to be the greatest obstacles to the Church's progress in our time.

1. Censoriousness

THE VIRTUE OF
GOD'S GESTAPO

"Do not judge others, so that God will not judge you—for God will judge you in the same way you judge others, and he will apply to you the same rules you apply to others. Why, then, do you look at the speck in your brother's eye and pay no attention to the log in your own eye? . . . You hypocrite! First take the log out of your own eye, and then you will be able to see clearly to take the speck out of your brother's eye."

Matthew 7:1–5, TEV

ROBERT BURNS SAT IN worship behind a lady who appeared to be the paradigm of elegance and poise. Then he saw a louse crawling on her shoulder. He immortalized that bug in his "Ode to a Louse." We've all heard the last line:

> O wad some Pow'r the Giftie gie us
> to see oursels as ithers see us.

Burns's point is obvious—we never look at ourselves as others look at us. We prefer our own self-portrait. Most of us would prefer to rewrite the lines, as Roger Shinn suggests, to read as follows:

> O wad some Pow'r to ithers gie
> to see myself as I see me.[1]

Whichever way we take it, the truth is that we humans are evaluating beings—we evaluate ourselves and we evaluate each other. However, we often find that we cannot stop with mere evaluation. We have to go further and either approve or condemn; and often we do the latter.

There is some urge within us to belittle the other guy, to

show him to be weaker or worse than ourselves. We are all somewhat like the church elder who was shown by his pastor that racial segregation was unbiblical. With a troubled air, he asked, "Well pastor, if I ain't better than a nigger, who am I better than?"

As noted earlier, this urge to condemn is especially powerful if we think of ourselves as being on *God's side*. There is not a more destructive force on earth than the religious person who condemns others out of a sense of service to God. The word *bigot* itself is a compound of the words "by God." [2]

It is this attitude of condemning others with God's blessing, that gives birth to the deadly virtue which I call *censoriousness*. Throughout the Church's history, it has repeatedly been considered virtuous to censor people's moral behavior and doctrinal thoughts. In every generation, the Church has honored a group of moral caretakers who might be called "God's Gestapo"—people who consider themselves guardians of the faith, the sniffers-out of heresy. As one wag put it, "Some religious leaders are of the opinion that the title 'Doctor of Divinity' really stands for 'Demon Detective.'" The notion is that the more steeped one becomes in matters of faith, the more he must become the moral magistrate of other people's lives.

Although it was just such a group who killed Jesus and just such a mentality against which Jesus warned us in Matthew 7, censoriousness has continued to be regarded as a virtue.

The word *censorious* comes from the Roman times when certain magistrates, called *censere*, were appointed to count the people, and supervise public morals. It was obviously a great honor to be named a *censere*, for it meant that one was morally a cut above others. The position was highly coveted and even came to be auctioned off at prodigious prices.

Evidently the concept of the *censere*, with its connotation of moral superiority, lapsed over into the Church, and we've never gotten rid of it. Even spiritual giants like John Calvin eventually became censors. In his later years, Calvin deprived one Servetus of the right to challenge orthodoxy, a right for which Calvin himself had fought long and hard. On an appointed day, Calvin stood on the outskirts of Geneva and supervised Servetus's execution by fire—all because Servetus had not gotten his doctrine of the Trinity quite right!

Our American forefathers fled the Old World in order to gain freedom from religious censorship; and not two generations later they adopted the same spirit of censoriousness, replete with floggings, drownings, and burnings. The Salem witch hunts are a monument to the deadly virtue of censoriousness.

Harry Emerson Fosdick wrote of his days as a youngster growing up in a godly home in New England. The religious perspective given to him by his parents was one of warmth and affection. God was viewed as a friend and helper, except when the itinerant preachers came to town to heat up the fires of hell for those who practiced such "sins" as card-playing, dancing, and theater-going. "I hold it everlastingly against them and all their kind," says Fosdick, "that as a young boy, because of their idiotic legalism, I refused my own father's invitation to see Edwin Booth in *Hamlet*." [3]

Censoriousness is not a stranger to the modern Church either. It is alive and well. There remains a belief that in order to be a committed Christian, one must join the ranks of God's Gestapo. Furthermore, a minister is so pressured to police unacceptable practices that even remaining silent about them is construed as tacit approval. "If you don't preach against it, you're for it" is a common attitude.

That being the case, I would like to say at this point that Christians should not only take a moral position in society, but they should also speak out on moral issues. I would also like to say that many Christians, past and present, are no doubt sincere in their desire to create a moral world. I am not advocating that Christians become mute on moral issues nor that they withdraw into a cocoon.

What I *am* suggesting is that censoriousness is the *wrong method* for producing a moral society. It accomplishes the precise opposite of its aim. That's why Jesus was so strongly opposed to it. Censoriousness was the method of the Pharisees, and Jesus' Sermon on the Mount was in a sense a protest against their method.

Why is censoriousness a deadly virtue? Why doesn't it work? Why did Jesus oppose it?

For one thing, it is deadly because of what it does to the censor. When I attempt to police the behavior or the beliefs of another person, I am forcing myself to do at least two things. First, I am forcing myself to stop focusing upon my sins and to start focusing upon someone else's. The more I look at your sins, the less I am aware of mine. Censoriousness forces me to blind myself to my own sins. Isn't this what Jesus meant when he asked, "Why do you condemn the speck in your brother's eye, and miss the log in your own eye?"

I'm reminded of the story about the zealot who was conducting a campaign against public nudity. He appeared before the local city council to advocate the passage of an ordinance regulating swimming attire in public pools. "Why, I drove past a pool last Sunday," he said, "and the girls were almost completely naked! The suits they were wearing were no bigger than two Band-aids! It was a moral disgrace!"

When one of the council members inquired as to what the boys had been wearing, the reformer had to admit that he hadn't noticed!

There is a subtle jealousy imbedded in censoriousness; a jealousy which parades itself in the name of righteousness. The reformer above was envious and didn't know it. He was motivated by the question "Why should others enjoy what I may not?" Someone has said that envy is the great leveler: if it cannot level things up, it levels them down. Whenever I see others enjoying what I would secretly like to enjoy, but am either too old or too cowardly to try, I may want to deprive them of their enjoyment—all in the name of moral reform. In reality, I am only blinding myself to my secret sin of envy. Lofton Hudson quotes a stanza from A. T. Lanta's poem, "Saints Who Have Never Been Caught." It speaks volumes concerning the effects of censoriousness upon the censor:

> I'm a sinner O Lord, and I know it . . . I'm weak, I
>   blunder, I fail . . .
> I'm tossed on life's stormy ocean; like ships embroiled in a
>   gale.
> I'm willing to trust in Thy mercy; to keep the command-
>   ments Thou'st taught . . .
> But deliver me, Lord, from the judgment . . . of Saints
>   who have never been caught.[4]

To put it another way, one of our favorite techniques for relieving ourselves from the guilt of our secret sins is to transfer those sins to someone else. You can often tell what a person feels most guilty about by listening to what he most loudly condemns in others.

The second thing I force myself to do when I assume the role of a censor is to take the place of God. At base, censoriousness is "unfaith." It is a refusal to trust that God is sufficiently able to create morality and to curb immorality.

I find it ironic that those who assume the role of censors often justify their posture with the claim of a great faith in God. Have they not read Acts 5? The Apostles were hauled before the Jewish council for preaching heresy. Their lives hung on the decision of the censors. One of the council members, Gamaliel, spoke out. In essence, he said, "Leave these men to God. If they are preaching man-made doctrines, they will fail. If they are preaching God-made doctrines, and we kill them, we will be fighting God." Censoriousness is a refusal to leave matters in God's hands.

Censoriousness is also a deadly virtue because of what it does to the one who is being censored. When a person is condemned for his errors, one of two things results, either of which is nonproductive.

First, condemnation can force a person to become a *rebel*. We humans have a built-in self-defense mechanism. When we're criticized, we rush to defend our position, *even if our position is wrong!* The attack doesn't help us change our position, it only entrenches us more deeply within it!

Have you noticed how "soft" Jesus was on the obvious sinners of his day? To the prostitutes, tax-collectors, and thieves, he gave a gentle, "Go thy way and sin no more." He did not conduct a frontal attack on these people. Perhaps he took this approach because he knew that a censorious attitude would only force them to defend their life-styles. In a word, he didn't want to make them rebels. Rebellion is caused by one of two motives: self-assertion or self-preservation. That is, some people rebel because they want power; they want to master others. They are driven by an insatiable desire to be "somebody." Others, however, rebel because rebellion is the only means by which they can preserve their self-identity. When they become overly censured by the system to which they are subject, rebellion is the only way out. It is either a matter of suffocation or resistance. Jesus refused to "suffocate" people by destroying their identity.

So, censoriousness produces rebels; but rebels are not free. Rebellion is simply another form of slavery—slavery to anger. A rebel is a protester and a destroyer. He stands against and he tears down. But afterward, he has to erect something in the place of what he has torn down. Rebellion is a halfway house to freedom.

Censoriousness, however, can have another destructive effect upon the one who is condemned. If it doesn't make him a rebel, it makes him a *robot*—a mindless, obedient machine who accepts orders without thought or question. He has no growth potential, no dialogue with God, discovers nothing new and wondrous.

Erich Fromm describes the nature of the human robot as *necrophilic,* a word meaning "love of the dead." [5] A necrophilic person loves order, organization, and mechanical, inert objects. He cannot abide change or newness or growth. He relies totally upon a system of laws which must be simply stated and easily defended. If one minute fragment of the system is violated, the whole system breaks down (in much the same way that an electrical generator can be shut down by the malfunction of a single circuit).

I don't think a more accurate description of the mentality of the Pharisee was ever written. Pharisaism was like all religious legalisms—its aim was to produce robots. And robots are not human. They have no capacity to question, to think, to discover, to create. They are slaves to the programs devised by the programmers.

The Danish philosopher Sören Kierkegaard described the robot-effect of censoriousness on the Church of his day in his satire "The Domestic Goose." (By the way, Kierkegaard was about as popular among his contemporaries as an Arab in a synagogue.)

"Try to imagine for a moment," says Kierkegaard, "that geese could talk—that they had so arranged things that they too had their divine worship and churchgoing.

Every Sunday they would meet together and a gander would preach.

The sermon was essentially the same each time—it told of the glorious destiny of the geese, of the noble end for which their maker had created them—and every time his name was mentioned all the geese curtsied and all the ganders bowed their heads. They were to use their wings to fly away to the distant pastures to which they really belonged; for they were only pilgrims on this earth.

The same thing happened each Sunday. Thereupon the

meeting broke up and they all waddled home, only to meet again next Sunday . . . and waddle off home again—but that was as far as they ever got. . . .

Among the geese there were several who looked ill and wan, and all the other geese said—there, you see what comes of taking flying seriously. It is all because they go about meditating on flying that they get thin and wan and are not blessed by the grace of God as we are. . . .

And so next Sunday, off they went to divine service, and the old gander preached of the glorious end for which their Maker (at that point all the geese curtsied and all the ganders bowed their heads) had created them, and why they were given wings." [6] The robot is no more free than the rebel.

Censoriousness is deadly because of what it does to the censor and because of what it does to the person who is being censored. It destroys the capacity of each to respond to God and to man.

I believe there is a better way to motivate persons to be moral. It was Jesus' way, yet we Christians seem to have all but forgotten it in our passion to police the world. Jesus' method for motivating people to be moral was the method of affirmation. That is, he looked inside of people until he found something good, and then he affirmed that goodness. He began with the assumption that every person had a "good spot" buried somewhere in his being. And he focused upon that good spot—watered it, fertilized it, nurtured it, and coaxed it to grow.

An example of Jesus' method is his encounter with the woman who was caught in the act of adultery.[7] The Jewish law said that she was to be executed by stoning, but the Romans forbade the Jews from executing wrongdoers. The story is well known: Jesus' enemies try to entrap him between Jewish law and Roman law. He asks them a question they can't answer; the crowd disperses and Jesus and the woman are left alone in the street.

What does Jesus do to help this woman? How does he motivate her toward mortality? First, he simply addresses her as a person—not as an object, not as a thing, not as the censors who have recently addressed her. He says, "Lady." How long had it been since anyone had called *her* a "lady"? She was used to hearing "slut" or "whore" but not "lady."

You see, Jesus found the "good spot." "There's a lady buried somewhere inside you," he was saying.

Next, he said, "Go your way and sin no more." Those seven words communicated two things to the woman. They said, "You can make a new beginning . . . right here . . . from this moment forward!" Then, they gave her something to reach for—a model, a goal, an inspiration.

Jesus showed her that she already had a spark of decency buried somewhere inside. He uncovered it and showed her she could take this potential and do something with it.

I first discovered how effective Jesus' method is from my seventy-year-old grandmother. We called her Big Mama, although she stood five feet tall and weighed no more than a hundred pounds.

Every October, Big Mama kept us for a month while my parents traveled. I was the apple of her eye. I could do no wrong.

As the October of my fifteenth year approached, I had a new car and had begun to keep the company of some of the town's more questionable characters. I made elaborate plans for the period of time when Big Mama would be keeping us.

The first Saturday night of her stay, I planned a grand adventure. A buddy and I had dates with the two girls most often mentioned in the football locker room. We also had certain "bottles" stashed. We had decided to consummate the evening by setting fire to an abandoned school house on the outskirts of town. Since Big Mama went to bed when the chickens did and slept as soundly as an anvil, and since she was so trusting, I felt that I had it made.

As I was dressing, Big Mama came into the room, sat down on the bed, and just looked at me with a strange smile on her face. Nervously, I said, "Why are you smiling?" "Oh, you wouldn't understand," she said. "Try me," I said. She continued to smile that knowing smile. "I was just thinking an old woman's thoughts," she mused. I was jittery now. "What thoughts?"

She paused for a moment, and said, "All right, I'll tell you. I was just sitting here thinking how good God has been to me. I've had five sons and daughters; and now God has let me live to see a fine grandson like you. Your parents can go away for a month and leave you with an old woman and never fear that you will misbehave."

On and on she went about how good I was and how good God had been to allow her to experience our relationship. *She ruined my night!*

I came home at eleven, sober as a judge. She had given me something to reach for. She made me "loyal to the royal" in myself. She found my "good spot" and appealed to it. She challenged me to live up to my potential. She affirmed her faith in my ability to do the good. And she herself stood as a model of inspiration for me. I knew I could act honorably because she acted honorably.

Let's suppose for a moment that she had used the method of censoriousness in trying to motivate me. Suppose she had said, "All of you youngsters are alike. . . . Always looking for an opportunity to jump over the traces. . . . You think I'm a naive old woman. . . . Well, I know what you and your sorry crowd are up to. . . . If you don't behave, your father will hear about this. . . . Etc., etc., etc."

Had Big Mama used all the tricks of the moral censor— condemnation, accusation, threats—what would have resulted? How would she have been affected? How would I have been affected?

Censoriousness would have led her to feel a certain sense of pride. She would have felt martyred. She would have gloried in the fact that she was willing to sacrifice a relationship with her grandson for the sake of her moral principles.

I, on the other hand, could have reacted in one of two ways. Her censoriousness could have made a rebel of me. I would have feigned innocence and hurt. I would have lied about my intentions, defended myself, and probably would have proceeded to carry out my plans for the evening anyway.

Of course, I could have responded in robot fashion and heeded her warnings. However, I would have resented her intrusion and probably would have looked forward to the day when no one could tell me what to do. She would have taken away my evening, but she wouldn't have taken away my desires to carry out what I had planned.

Censoriousness can prevent people from breaking the law, but it cannot take away their desire to break the law. That's why it is a deadly virtue! That's why Jesus and Paul went to great lengths to condemn legalism. A goodness that is based upon keeping the law for the law's sake does not produce a happy society. We must keep the law because we want to, not because we're afraid not to!

Censoriousness will not produce a moral society. It will only produce self-righteous Pharisees, robots, and rebels. It is not a Christian virtue. God has not called us to sniff out the wrong in others and to punish them. He has called us to sniff out the good in them and to point them to what they can become in God's grace.

> *Why, then, do you look at the speck*
> *in your brother's eye?*

2. Permissiveness

THE VIRTUE OF
THE FREE-LOADER

"Do not give what is holy to dogs—they will only turn and attack you. Do not throw your pearls in front of pigs—they will only trample them underfoot."

Matthew 7:6, TEV

CENSORIOUSNESS REPRESENTS an extremist position; but every extreme has its opposite, and it is the opposite of censoriousness that we shall address now. I call it *permissiveness*.

Permissiveness is an attitude characterized by the opinion that it is wrong to take an absolute position on any subject or issue—except, of course, the position that it is wrong to take absolute positions. It worships what Nicholas Von Hoffman calls "the great Mush God." "The great Mush God," say Von Hoffman, "has no theology to speak of, being a cream of wheat deity. The Mush God has no particular credo, no tenets of faith, nothing that would make it difficult for believer and non-believer alike to lower one's head when the temporary chairman tells us that Reverend, Rabbi, Father, Mufti, So-and-so will lead us in an innocuous prayer; for this God of public occasions is not a jealous God. You can even invoke him to start a hookers' convention and he/she or it won't be offended. . . . God of Rotary, God of Optimists Club, Protector of the Buddy System, the Mush God is the lord of secular ritual . . . a serviceable God whose laws aren't chiseled on tablets but written on sand, amenable to amendment, qualification and erasure." [1]

33

In the modern Christian world, permissiveness often masquerades itself as tolerance. It is considered virtuous to condemn nothing and stand for everything, for the sake of being regarded as tolerant. But permissiveness is not tolerance at all. To be tolerant means to be receptive to all forms of truth. A tolerant person refuses to prejudge any claim or issue until he has investigated and tested it. He also refuses to condemn *persons* who happen to hold different opinions. However, this does not mean that he has no convictions himself. One can be tolerant and maintain deep convictions at the same time. To be tolerant means to be teachable and flexible.

A permissive person, however, refrains from testing anything. His motto is "live and let live," "anything goes." His most ardent fear is that he will be thought narrow-minded by his peers. Out of a sincere desire to be accepted by all, he embraces everything and stands for nothing. He is somewhat like the preacher who was requested by his congregation to deliver a sermon on sin. Knowing that his parishioners were locked in a dispute over the right and wrong of such issues as drinking, smoking, dancing, and extramarital sex, he said: "What I have to say about sin can be summed up in three words: I'm against it!"

Permissiveness not only loves approval, it also loves the convenience of neutrality. Nothing is quite so convenient as not having to take a stand, and quite often one is rewarded in the church for being neutral. A colleague told me of a man in his congregation who absolutely refused to take a position on any issue. The result was that he quickly rose to prominence in the leadership of the church. He established a reputation of impartiality and was respected by all.

In reality, his strategy was to refrain from ever voting on a proposal. Therefore, if the proposal turned out to be unwise, he could say he had been against it, and if it proved to be wise, he could say that he had been for it.

One evening, the church was called into session to decide

whether to put a new roof on the sanctuary. My friend called for the vote by saying, "All those in favor, please rise, and all those against, please remain seated." The man looked about, rocked to and fro in his seat, and finally rose to a half-crouch!

Permissiveness indeed has its advantages in the Church today. It seems so humane, so civil, so fair-minded to bless everything and condemn nothing. In fact, it seems in tune with the spirit of Jesus' words that we used to introduce the preceding chapter. "Don't censor! Don't judge others! Don't condemn!," he tells us in Matthew 7:1–5. If those five verses were taken in isolation from the rest of what he said in the Sermon on the Mount, one could pretty well claim that the Church should refrain from challenging any and all behavior.

But let us go on to verse 6: "Don't give what is holy to dogs —they will turn and attack you; don't throw your pearls in front of pigs—they will only trample them underfoot."

What is this? First he says, "Don't condemn! Don't censor!," and then he says, "Don't expose yourself to certain modes of behavior—they will only destroy you!" On the one hand, Jesus urges tolerance, and on the other he urges discrimination!

Is this a contradiction? Some biblical scholars think so.[2] They believe that an ancient bigot inserted verse 6 because he couldn't tolerate Jesus' order against censoriousness in verses 1–5.

I believe that verse 6 is totally in keeping with the mind-set of Jesus. He had a balanced way of looking at things. He was neither an extremist nor an impractical idealist. He added the words of verse 6 precisely to guard against an extremist interpretation of verses 1–5. In other words, he wanted to warn us that there is a point at which broadmindedness becomes an *excuse for condoning everything and standing for nothing*.

There are numerous evidences that permissiveness holds an honored position in the Church today. For example, it is not uncommon to find an article by a leading clergyman next to the nude centerfold in a "skin" magazine. Some theologians seem to be hard at work to produce systems that will allow a person to believe and do whatever he likes without violating Christian principles.

Such exercises remind me of the story which came out of the famous Boxer Rebellion in China near the turn of the century. The rebels would march each of their captives to the executioner's block and ask if he were a Christian. If he said yes, they lopped off his head. If he said no, they released him. A bishop was brought to the block and asked the crucial question. "If you will give me a few moments," he said, "I think I can come up with an answer that will satisfy both sides."

How does permissiveness come to be regarded as a Christian virtue? I think the answer has to do with an overall trend that is sweeping our Western culture. For the past few years, the Western world has been experiencing a rebellion against the moral strategy of Puritanism. In many ways the Puritan moral code used censoriousness as its method for producing a moral society. Puritanism held a rather low view of man. He was considered totally depraved and incapable of the good. His sexual lust was seen as a living proof of his depraved nature. Therefore, sex became almost synonymous with sin.

For a time, the Puritan method produced mostly robots, but eventually it produced a horde of rebels. (The publishers of *Playboy, Penthouse,* and other such magazines did not create the sexual revolution, they simply cashed in on it.) The society, aided by the pill and antibiotics that removed the two *practical* negatives from free sex, rebelled en masse. As the tide of public opinion rose against the Church's traditional ethic, the Church panicked. Its attitude seemed to become, "If you can't whip 'em, join 'em." Permissiveness became a virtue.

Meanwhile, the same process occurred in the field of Christian philosophy. Under the onslaught of scientific technology, logical positivism, and psychological determinism, the Church gave in. For example, I spent most of my four years in graduate school reading Christian intellectuals who were trying to figure a way to believe in Jesus' resurrection without saying that he biologically rose from the dead!

In a word, permissiveness became a virtue in the Church, both ethically and intellectually, as a result of the Church's desire to have the best of both worlds—a world dominated by man, and a world dominated by God.

Herein lies the clue to why permissiveness is such a deadly virtue. Once a Christian succumbs to the belief that he can have an "arrangement" with God, he's in trouble. "No one can serve two masters," said Jesus. Anything with two heads is a monster.

I can testify firsthand to the subtleties of permissiveness. When I first began to pursue the ministry as a vocation, I was like most "new" Christians. I wanted very much to prove my worthiness to the saints. In our denomination, fledgling ministers are affectionately known as "preacher-boys." With my Christian conversion only six months behind me, I enrolled in a Baptist school as a preacher-boy.

Almost immediately I noticed that the world of the preacher-boy had its own special categories. There were certain "preacher-boyisms" that went along with the vocation. For example, the preacher-boys used taglines such as "Praise the Lord" and "God willing," to be inserted at appropriate moments during conversation. They were also expected to be the highest examples of moral rectitude. To laugh at an off-color joke—or at anything else, for that matter—was considered highly suspect. Preacher-boys even talked peculiarly, articulating their words in a special way. The word *Jesus* was always pronounced with a double "ee", for example. One more thing—I noticed that preacher-boys seemed to have an unwritten obligation to offend as many sinners as possible. The more aggressive one was with nonbelievers, the more standing he held in the community.

I dived into the preacher-boy world with enthusiasm. I was a full-fledged devotee of God's Gestapo, out to uncover and convict the enemies of the Reich. Through college and most of seminary, I employed all the mannerisms and "bulldog-matism" I could muster. The formal education I was receiving smacked of a "preacher factory," designed to turn out products according to patented specifications. Rather than a market-place of ideas where one is exposed to multiple viewpoints and given the freedom to choose without recriminations, one view-point was presented and reinforced. Failure to comply with this viewpoint brought with it the stamp of "Liberal," and in my denomination the scarlet letter is an "L."

I would have none of that. I was a faithful soldier of the cause, with ambitions to pastor a huge church and speak at all of the denominational conferences.

After receiving a doctorate, I assumed my first pastorate in one of the most conservative areas of our state. The church flourished and my star seemed to be rising in the denomina-tion. However, my efforts as a legalist and censor began to turn sour. I was coming to a crisis of conscience, because I was beginning to see that in order to be a true legalist, I would also have to be a fraud.

I couldn't keep all of the rules. I was human. But preachers are not permitted that luxury! So, my only alternatives were either to pretend that I was keeping the rules or to reduce the rules to those I could keep!

I was also doomed to frustration because I was shutting myself off from God's forgiving process. It happened this way: Every time I discovered a new sin in my life, I would hide it and work to overcome it. When I conquered it, a new one would crop up. My sins were like Johnson grass—even if I cut one off below the surface, another one cropped up somewhere else.

In a word, I was trying to *work* for my salvation. The Law is a cruel master. I couldn't admit that I was human and I didn't have enough fingers to plug all the leaks in my right-eousnes. I completely lost contact with God's forgiving love.

Then I had what I call my "second conversion." I redis-covered Paul's letter to the Romans. We don't want to believe what Paul says about God's forgiveness in that letter. As Carlisle Marney says, "We've spent twenty centuries trying to tone him down." [3]

Briefly stated, Paul says that God forgives *all* our sins— the ones we committed in the past *and the ones we will commit in the future!* We *are* forgiven!

The immediate effect of this discovery was a new freedom to be me. I stopped pretending, hiding, and playing the game I had been playing. I admitted my humanness openly. If I had doubts, I acknowledged them. I began to like myself again. I stopped talking like a preacher, and looking like a preacher, and smiling like a preacher.

The reaction of the people was mixed. Those who didn't want a human for a pastor, became hostile; actually they were frightened, and hostility is the child of fear. Others responded eagerly. People who had rejected the Church began to return to worship. Soon the Sunday services were filled. Some came out of anger and took notes to use against me at a later time. Some came because they had longed to hear a minister who shared their struggles and doubts and brokenness. Others were simply curious.

At this point, something subtle began to take place in my life. I couldn't see it then, but I can now. For one thing, I began to retaliate against the traditional conservatives who attacked me. I resorted to shock-tactics. I took great satis-faction in "afflicting the comfortable." I preached on every far-out, exotic viewpoint I could find. I courted fights at every corner.

At the same time, I also began to use my honesty as a tool to gain sympathy from the nontraditionalists. I went to great lengths to show what a "regular guy" I was. I inserted cuss words into my vocabulary and told dirty jokes in the appropriate circles. I also took pains to refrain from any expression that would indicate that I was "spiritual."

Here's the point: *Whereas I was formerly ashamed to admit that I was human, I now became ashamed to admit that I walked with God.* A free-spirit can aggrandize himself by bragging on his sins, just as a Pharisee can aggrandize himself by bragging on his righteousness.

In a word, I had gone from one extreme to the other—from censoriousness to permissiveness. It took me a while to awaken to the realization that my new virtues were as deadly as my former ones. In fact, it took the hurting of a lot of people and a move to a new pastorate. My new pastorate had the outward appearances of all I was hoping for at that stage of my life. It was a university church and had established itself as open and socially aware. It was the first white Baptist church in Texas to integrate racially (in 1950, *before* the Supreme Court ruling on school desegregation). It was also the first Southern Baptist church in Texas to ordain women as deacons. I was grateful that all the battles with legalism had already been fought before I got there. I could "do my thing" candidly and without fear.

Was I in for a surprise! I soon discovered that many of the deacons in the church contributed little or no money to the church's ministries, nor did they hold any other positions of service. They simply met once a month to set policies and check out the staff's performance!

There was very little Bible study going on either. Many felt that they had graduated to more challenging pursuits. The members of the first Sunday school class I attended were studying a book on existentialism that I had used as a text in a graduate philosophy seminar.

The church buildings were literally falling down. The city building inspectors were even threatening to condemn one of them.

As the months passed, the church's personality began to take shape for me. A handful of faithful souls, most of them older and more pietistic than the majority of the members, were carrying the church with their tithes, their offerings, their prayers, and their witness. *Most of the free-thinkers, however, were also free-loaders!* They talked a great game; they were loving and accepting of their pastor and friends, but they were lacking in daily Christian discipline and devotion.

Furthermore, when it came to establishing new programs and trying new ministries, these so-called "free people" tended to be as close-minded as any legalist. They were as cliquish as the fundamentalists I had been battling in West Texas. In fact, I found myself praying for God to send us a few of those guilt-ridden, narrow-minded souls who believed in showing up on time and pitching in to pay the church's bills!

At this point I experienced a "third conversion." I saw that the Christian way has to be a "way of the middle." If it leans too far to the right, it lapses into censoriousness. If it leans too far to the left, it lapses into permissiveness.

Let me come at this discussion another way by using the cross and the resurrection of Jesus as a model. One brand of Christianity offers people a cross without a resurrection. It believes that God's love must be earned through the bearing of great burdens and through suffering. Fear and guilt are the chief threads in its fabric.

Another brand of Christianity offers resurrection without a cross. God's love has no responsibilities attached to it. It is cheap to receive and cheap to maintain.

The first brand of Christianity is characterized by censoriousness; the second brand is characterized by permissiveness. Jesus' brand of Christianity is the cross-resurrection brand. God's love is freely given, but it is not cheap. Those who receive it are forgiven, and they are free to be who they are without fear. But they are not free to be irresponsible. The way to the resurrection is by way of the cross.

Censoriousness knows nothing of grace. Permissiveness knows only of cheap grace, yet we persist in thinking of these two noxious attitudes as virtues.

Several years ago, I was leading a series of services as guest speaker at a local church, and the pastor wanted me to explain how to become a Christian to a group of seventh graders. We gathered in the church parlor, and after I had told a few anecdotes to break the ice, I began my explanation. I held up a half-dollar and said, "Would anyone here like to have this?"

Of course, they all nodded affirmatively. I summoned a tow-headed lad to the front and placed the coin in his hand. "This is yours," I said. He looked suspicious. "What do I have to do for it?" he inquired. "Nothing," I said. "It is yours with no strings attached! I'm giving it to you because I love you." "Baloney," he exclaimed. "Nobody gets nothin' for nothin'. Besides, how could you love me? You don't even know me!"

Everybody laughed. I was embarrassed. Obviously, I had planned to make the point that God gives us eternal life with no strings attached. All we have to do is reach out and take it. But the bravado of that little boy showed me something I hadn't realized before.

"You're right," I injected. "I don't know you, but God does, and he loves you. And you're right on the first count, too. Nobody gets nothin' for nothin'! So, tell you what, I will give you this fifty-cent piece, if you will come and live with me and be my son from now on." Without hesitation, he shot back, "Make it a million, and I'll come!"

The audience guffawed. My attempt at child evangelism was a disaster. I never did regain their attention. But I'm fond of the analogy nonetheless. God gives us life, freely. We cannot earn his love. But the clincher is that we are to forsake our securities and become children in his household. Those who see censoriousness as a virtue would tell us that we must earn God's gifts. Those who regard permissiveness as a virtue would have us believe that we can receive God's gifts and not change residences.

3. Childishness

THE VIRTUE OF
THE SERVICELESS SERVANT

"There was once a man who was going down from Jerusalem to Jericho when robbers attacked him, stripped him, and beat him up, leaving him half dead. It so happened that a priest was going down that road; but when he saw the man, he walked on by on the other side. In the same way a Levite . . . walked on by on the other side. But a Samaritan who was traveling that way came upon the man, and when he saw him, his heart was filled with pity. He went over to him, poured oil and wine on his wounds and bandaged them; then he put the man on his own animal and took him to an inn, where he took care of him. The next day he took out two silver coins and gave them to the innkeeper. "Take care of him," he told the innkeeper, "and when I come back this way, I will pay you whatever else you spend on him."

Luke 10:30–35, TEV

TEN THOUSAND YEARS from now, if a graduate student wants to write a thesis depicting twentieth-century American values, he should begin by researching how we buy and sell consumer products. If he were to begin with the names we assign to various goods, he would discover that *Joy, Bold,* and *Zest* are soaps; that *Sure, Secret,* and *Right Guard* are deodorants; that *Gusto* and *Christian Brothers* are alcoholic drinks; that *Power* is a candy bar; that *Merit, Fact,* and *Vantage* are cigarettes; that *Brut* is a cologne and *My Sin* a perfume; that a *Hero* is a sandwich and a *Free Spirit,* a bra; and that *The Real Thing* is a soda pop.

Then he should do an in-depth analysis of television commercials. He should notice that the admen of Madison Avenue use three dominant motifs in marketing consumer goods. The first is *fear of punishment.* The message conveyed in this genre of advertising is, "If you don't buy our product, you will suffer dire consequences." Here's an example: The camera finds husband and wife asleep in the bed. He is suddenly stricken with a hacking cough which awakens the wife. With wagging finger, she says, "One more sneeze and I'm leaving! Naughty boy! You've been taking that popular liquid cough suppres-

45

sant again! How many times must I tell you that what you need is the capsule with the tiny time-release formula!" Now comes the clincher. "I don't want to leave you," she threatens, "so, give your cold to Contac, and lets both get some sleep." The message: *If you don't take Contac, you will lose my love. . . . You will be punished!* Fear of punishment is the motivational technique behind dozens of commercials, including many of those that appear during children's prime viewing hours. Join your four-year-old some Saturday morning and note the subtle threats injected during the cartoon fare.

Hope of reward is another of the dominant motifs employed by the admen. The word is: "If you buy our product, you will reap great benefits." Flick on the tube any time and you will notice the promise of fantastic rewards for the cost of some cosmetic or gadget.

Here's a stunningly attractive creature with hungry eyes, who says, "All my men wear English Leather . . . every one of them," which being interpreted, means: "Buy English Leather and you will become *my* man."

Then there's the soft drink that promises to "add life." And, you guessed it, *"Everybody* wants a little life!" Or, the popular foreign cars, 72 percent of which are owned by people with college degrees—the remaining 28 percent being "just plain smart." In our rational moments we would never be vain enough to believe that we could lengthen our lives one minute or deepen our intelligence one whit by purchasing soda pop or a hunk of mechanized tin. But the admen know about our lurking fears of death and dumbness. They know that if there is some way—even a silly way—to tie the promises of lengthy life and increased intelligence to their products, we'll remember those products when we get ready to buy.

The third motif of TV advertising is known as the *good-person* motif. The pitch is, "If you want to be regarded as a good person, buy our product." Caricatures of "good-persons" are hammered into our consciousness. For instance, a "good-person" has dry underarms, no dandruff, antiseptic breath, smooth cheeks, a flat belly, and wouldn't be caught dead with ring around the collar. He is also bullish on America, and listens religiously to E. F. Hutton.

Norman Douglas once said, "You can tell the ideals of a nation by its advertisements." That, in a nutshell, is the point of the above. The names of the products we consume and the methods the advertisers use to motivate us to buy them would lead our future graduate student to conclude that at this stage in our history most of us were living our lives on what I'm calling in this chapter "a level of childishness."

A child, for all his cuddly warmth and refreshing innocence, is basically self-centered. I'm not using the terms "childish" and "self-centered" in a condemning, judgmental sense. I'm using them to point to the fact that a child sees himself as *separate*—as a self over against all other selves. He does not see himself as being part of a community. He feels that he is alone, unto himself. He has an "I-against-world" perspective.

For example, a child has no altruistic loyalties to others. His attachment to his parents is based upon his need for protection and security. If a small child's parents leave him in the care of others for a few months, he forgets the parents almost completely. A German friend once described to me the experience of living through the Allied bombings of Berlin near the end of World War II. I asked him if he were afraid to die, and he said, "No, not really. It may sound strange, but my fear was that my parents would be killed and that there would be no one left to take care of me." The primary concern of a child is, "What will happen to *me?*"

When we seek to motivate a child, we use the techniques which most appeal to his egocentricity. *And the three most effective of these techniques are: fear of punishment, hope of reward, and "good-person."* We mold a small child's character by punishing him, rewarding him, and praising him. These are effective legitimate techniques to use with a child, *while* he is a child.

However, as the child grows older, he learns (or should learn) that there are other centers of being in the world whom he must consider and give his talents to. When he begins to recognize this, we begin to teach him that there are other reasons for being honest, considerate, and other desirable qualities besides fear of punishment, hope of reward, and good-person.

But, has our society grown beyond the childish level? Obviously, the admen do not think so. They have rather lucrative proof that the majority of society responds to childish, "me"-level motivations. I once heard the president of one of the leading advertising agencies in America say that all television commercials are aimed at a ten- to fourteen-year-old level of understanding!

There is other evidence to support the conclusion that ours is a society which has not grown beyond the me-level of motivation. Consider the common attitude that the worst thing about sin is getting caught. When a child does something wrong, his chief concern is not the act itself but the punishment he will receive if his wrongdoing is found out. Given his childish egotism, he evaluates his actions totally from the standpoint of what will happen to him. He is not concerned with the effects of his actions upon others or the world. He is not yet mature enough to perceive that his actions have a broader effect. Thus, his main concern lies in getting caught, in being exposed, in receiving punishment. The sin as he sees it does not lie in the act but in its exposure to the public eye.

An amazing number of adults in our society seem to think the same way: "It's okay as long as one doesn't get caught." As a minister, I often encounter this way of thinking in people who use profanity. They feel quite free to spice their conversations with four-letter words until they discover that I am a clergyman. Immediately they apologize, clean up their language, and start behaving with a peculiar "saintly" air. It is obvious that their use of profanity doesn't bother them nearly so much as having been caught doing it in the presence of a minister.

Consider the last few presidents who have served our nation. Recent stories apparently reveal that several of them at least abused the public trust, if not committing outright crimes. Yet, only one got caught with a "smoking gun" in his hand. He now stands disgraced and scorned, but the others enjoy the blessings of a fond remembrance from the nation. One got caught and the others didn't. One is guilty and the others are not. A child feels that the worst thing about sin is getting caught. So does a childish society.

The childish motives that seem to regulate so much of our society's values and actions also govern the values and actions of many churchgoers. A large number of churchmen are motivated by the same three motives: fear of punishment, hope of reward, and good-person. In fact childishness has come to be regarded in many Christian circles as a virtue! It has become quite respectable to fulfill religious obligations out of a fear of hell, a hope for heaven, and the title of good-person! In a word, many of us have made a virtue out of religious service whose chief concern is "What will happen to me?" Some of the fastest growing religious groups in America are putting the me-level motivations to good use. The "turn-or-burn" strategy is making quite a comeback, for example. People are not being called to join God's mission to heal a broken world; they are being offered an asbestos sanctuary from the fires of hell—an escape from impending punishment.

Then there's the "heaven-on-a-dollar-a-week" plan. It is enjoying record "sales" these days, its success being tied to the "turn-or-burn" stratagem mentioned above. First, people must be convinced, through exotic applications of the Scriptures to current world events, that the end of the world is imminent.

With that settled, they are offered heaven as a reward for responding to Christ. But heaven is offered at bargain prices. The down-payment is church affiliation; the balance may be paid in easy installments of church attendance, acceptable public moral behavior, and a dollar a week.

The third Church strategy being aimed at me-level motivations is the "Sacred-Society-of-Secluded-Saints" strategy, or the "4-S" strategy. The idea is that while one awaits the End in one's asbestos sanctuary and pays the weekly installments on heaven, one can become a good-person by separating himself from the sinful world. One cannot associate with those outside the "4-S" or he will lose the status of good-person.

How could so many people be drawn to a church that employs strategies like those mentioned above? How could people embrace something *that foreign* to Jesus' strategy? The answer is that such strategies always give results whenever religious devotion is reduced to the me-level. Once a person's chief motivation for religious service becomes centered in the question, "What will happen to me?" his religion will inevitably be dominated by fear of punishment, hope of reward, and good-person.

Now, there is no question but that the three me-level motives have some validity when it comes to presenting the gospel to those who do not know Jesus Christ. In a spiritual sense, unbelievers *are* children; and hell, heaven, and respectability are legitimate reasons for embracing God. However, once a person becomes a child of God, if he remains on the me-level—indeed, if he sees it virtuous to remain there—he becomes in reality what I call a *fixated* child of God! And a fixated Christian has no growth potential. He cannot grow because he is tied to the past. He cannot "open up" to the future.

The British preacher, Watkinson, tells of strolling along a beach one day with his grandson. They met an old man and greeted him politely, whereupon the old fellow began to curse them vilely. They were frightened and confused until a by-stander explained that the old man was suffering from sun-stroke. The little boy didn't quite catch the appropriate word, and as they walked away, he said to Watkinson, "Grandpa, I hope you never suffer from a *sunset.*"

A fixated Christian suffers from "sunset." He cannot see the dawn of God's activities in the world, of God's continuing forgiveness, of God's "new" revelations. That's why childish-ness—governing one's Christian life by the three childish mo-tives—is a deadly virtue.

Look at other ways in which childishness kills the Church. *For one thing, a childish Christian can never become a re-productive Christian.* In one sense, a child is a liability, a de-pendent. He requires constant attention and care. His every problem and hurt must be attended by his parents. He cannot feed himself, clothe himself, or even recognize danger.

Translate this image to the childish Christian. Our churches are filled with people who view the Church as parent. (Usu-ally, the clergy and the Church are seen as synonymous.) They go to the Church in order to be fed, stroked, coddled, and protected (some even come to be spanked for their way-wardness). The Church is a place where they get served, not a vehicle through which they serve God and others.

The result is that our churches have become child-care centers, staffed by parent-figures (professional clergymen and a few lay-persons) who bear the burden of servicing the flock on a twenty-four-hour basis. The only reproduction that takes place is in the form of the "new babies" born as a result of the me-level gospel that is being preached.

Babies don't reproduce babies; only adults can procreate. Almost every church reflects the same pattern: a few adults who procreate, and a host of "children" who cry out every time the Pablum disagrees with them, the building is too hot or too cold, the pew is too hard, or the parents are slow to respond to wet diapers in the middle of the night

A childish Christian cannot turn his life outward and become God's partner in healing a broken world. He can only
demand service, he cannot give service. *A childish church
cannot be a New Testament church.* Volumes have been written on what it means to be the New Testament Church. I do
not wish to add another one. Therefore, let me say only this:
(1) the Church is people; (2) these people are the people
whom God intends to use to redeem the world; (3) therefore, the people of God are to be servants.

If the above description of the Church is true, people who
live on a me-level of motivation cannot be the Church. In
order to be servants, people must be motivated by something
other than their own comfort and security.

Childishness also has a debilitating effect on the clergyman.
The biblical concept of the minister is that of an equipper. His
task is to equip the saints, and most professional ministers
enter their vocation with the conscious motive of wanting to
fulfill this role. Later, some discover that subconsciously they
became ministers also because they wanted to earn God's approval. They had a low self-image which they wanted to improve by being servants. In short, all ministers embrace their
vocations with the *conscious* motive of wanting to *give* love,
and some, like myself, later discover that they were also driven
by the *subconscious* desire to receive approval.

However, whether a person becomes a minister to get or
to give love, the childishness I've been describing is equally
devastating. The minister who wants to give love discovers
that his parishioners are not interested in his equipping them
to be lay ministers. They want a "creature of response" who is
always at their beck and call. Most of these ministers either
drop out or live with the perpetual feeling that they are "kept
persons" who are not fulfilling their calling. Recently, one
colleague told me, "I am a whore, a spiritual dilettante who is
paid by the congregation to serve up favors at their beck and

call. They don't want me to equip them to become ministers; they want a well-kept creature of response."

The ministers who are out to get love and approval are even more plagued. Either they wear themselves to exhaustion by trying to respond to every request, or they allow themselves to become the parent-figures which the "children" demand. They find that their position can be solidified by keeping the children "childish." They become the chief proponents of Christian childishness, constantly preaching fear of punishment, hope of reward, and good-person as the reasons for doing what they say.

In short, childishness is deadly to the clergyman because it can force him either to quit, or to exhaust himself in frustration, or to reinforce childishness as a Christian virtue. Fortunately, however, these are not his only alternatives. He can pursue another course. It is difficult but it can be done. He can stand his ground and defend his role as an equipper. He can refuse to be cowed by those who see childishness as a virtue, and he can teach his people "a better way."

In practical terms, how is this accomplished? How does one get the saints to begin to move beyond serving God out of fear of punishment, hope of reward, and good-person? The only place to begin is with a reexamination of the New Testament. And the place to begin in the New Testament is with what Jesus taught about the true motives for Christian service.

Let's take one example of Jesus' teaching on why people are to serve God—the parable of the Good Samaritan (Luke 19:25–37). A religious "expert" tries to stump Jesus by asking what one must do to receive eternal life. Jesus answers, "What do the Scriptures say?" The man replies, "You must love God . . . and you must love your neighbor as yourself." "You're right," says Jesus. Then the "expert" comes at him with another question, one that is designed to throw him off— "Who is my neighbor?"

Jesus answers with a parable. A man who was traveling was attacked by robbers and left to die in the ditch. At different intervals, a priest and a Levite (religious lawyer) passed by, saw the man in distress, and left him without rendering aid. Then a Samaritan came by, gave him first aid, took him to an inn, and paid his bill. "Who was the man's neighbor?" asks Jesus. "The Samaritan," replied the expert. Jesus says, "You go, then, and do the same."

Look at this story in light of what we've said about childishness. The priest and Levite were extremely religious persons, but their religion was of the me-level variety. Their concern was, "If I help this man, *what will happen to me?* I could be hurt. The guy may be a decoy [fear of punishment]. I have nothing to gain by helping him. What can I get out of helping some derelict? [hope of reward]. If I help him, or if I don't, . . . it won't affect what others think of me. I'm already considered a *good-person.*" The man in the ditch did not qualify for service, as they saw it, because his well-being had no bearing on their me-level of action.

The Samaritan, however, was operating on a different level. Call it the we-level, if you will. His question was not, "If I help this man, what will happen to me?" It was, "If I don't help this man, what will happen to *him?*" His motive for service was larger than his concern for the "me." I believe he realized that what happened to the needy person, in a sense, was happening also to himself. He somehow realized that in God's world, what happens to one happens to all. If the man were hurting, then he was hurting, too.

But the Samaritan was not totally selfless. He didn't aid the injured man because the welfare of others was his *only* concern. He aided the man because he saw that by helping others he was also helping himself—because others were part of *himself!*

Jesus didn't say, "Love others *more* than you love yourself"; he said, "Love others *as* you love yourself."

No Christian can serve beyond the childish level of self-service until he realizes that he and others are of the same flesh, until he can say "we." I heard Andrew Young say that racial prejudice is really the symptom of a deeper human tendency to discriminate against anyone who is different from us, whether it be a difference of skin pigmentation, of dress, of language, or of hair style. He said that we tend to look at others who differ from us as *threats* to our existence. What Christianity has to offer is the unique revelation that all men are in truth *complements* of our existence.[1]

Childishness knows nothing of complementarity. It is based upon the belief that we are different and separate from others; therefore, they are threats to our existence. It is also based upon the assumption that the church is an organization designed primarily to improve one's spiritual standing with God. Many people go to a church for the same reason that they go to an auto mechanic when their car is broken, or a doctor when they are ill. The church is the place where one gets repaired and cured. The very idea of the church's being a community where one is equipped to heal and repair the world, and by so doing receives his own healing, is a foreign idea.

A faithful churchgoer once said to me, "I come to church for three reasons: I'm afraid not to; I want to go to heaven; and I like to be liked. If I said there were other reasons, I'd be lying." Unfortunately, I fear that he was speaking for a host of people who see childishness as a Christian virtue. His motives are healthy for Christian babes; but for Christian adults they represent the style of the serviceless servants.

4. Exhibitionism

THE VIRTUE OF
THE HOLY HAWKER

"Make certain you do not perform your religious duties in public so that people will see what you do. If you do these things publicly, you will not have any reward from your Father in heaven.

"So, when you give something to the needy, do not make a big show of it, as the hypocrites do in the houses of worship and on the streets. They do it so that people will praise them. . . .

"When you pray, do not be like the hypocrites! They love to stand up and pray in the houses of worship and on the street corners, so that everybody will see them. . . .

"And when you fast, do not put on a sad face as the hypocrites do. They neglect their appearance so that everyone will see that they are fasting. I assure you, they have already been paid in full."

Matthew 6:1–2, 5, 16, TEV

MY WIFE AND I were walking down Bourbon Street in New Orleans. The evening session of the denominational conference we were attending had just adjourned and the sidewalks were jammed with clergymen from all over America. I'm afraid we all looked like gawking country-folk come to town on Saturday night. This was not our world. The cab drivers were circulating the story about the Baptist who came to New Orleans with the Ten Commandments and a ten-dollar bill, and broke neither one!

The hawkers at the strip joints knew that business would be nil, so they had evidently decided to make the best of it. They stood by the doors of the clubs and made up new routines. One was shouting: "Come right in, folks! The show's about to begin. If you don't like our girls, there's a prayer meeting going on in the back room!"

Another said: "See our ex-choirgirl, folks! She's guaranteed to revive you! Step right in. . . . Recommended by Billy Graham!"

Needless to say, their sales pitches offended the saints not a little. There was much gnashing of teeth. Had there been any loose stones lying about, I fear that the hawkers wouldn't have lasted very long.

However, some of us took their spiels good-naturedly. I knew how the hawkers viewed us. We were aliens from another world. We wanted nothing to do with their product or *them*. Their natural reaction was to chide us and scorn us. So, I decided simply to laugh with them, as we sauntered along the street.

Suddenly, a young girl sprang directly in front of me. "Do you think that's funny!" she shouted. I was too stunned to reply. "You're going to burn in a devil's hell for laughing at this blasphemy!" she went on.

"Young lady," I said, "I'm not laughing at God. I'm laughing at this ridiculous scene." She interrupted me, "Do you know Jesus?" she said. "Have you ever accepted him as your Lord and Savior? Been washed in his blood? Surrendered to him?"

By now, a crowd had gathered around us. Quietly, I said, "Ma'am, I am a minister, and—" She broke in, "I don't care if you're president of the world; do you know Jesus?"

About this time a professional evangelist, whom I had known back in school, stepped up and arrested her attack. "Yes, he knows Jesus," said the evangelist, referring to me. "Old George here is a friend of mine from way back." (He missed my name.)

The girl was one of a group of youngsters whom the evangelist had recruited to come to New Orleans to "witness for Christ" during the conference. Business had been as slow for them as for the hawkers at the strip joints. Neither group was scoring very well, so apparently *both had done the same thing*—they had resorted to a kind of offensive overbearingness in order to justify their existence.

There was not a whit of difference between what the hawkers were doing and what the witnesses were doing! Both were trying to capture "aliens" with shock tactics! Their motives were different, but their methods were the same—and so were the results, I might add.

To me, this incident and others like it raise the question of how Christians are to go about reaching non-Christians. There is no doubt that every Christian is called by God to disciple others. Evangelism is the lifeblood of the Church. A living church must be a witnessing church. The world cannot be changed until people are changed; and people can be changed only when they hear the gospel. So, there is no question as to the absolute necessity of witnessing. But there is a question as to how it is to be done.

There is a point at which witnessing becomes an overbearing, "ram-it-down-the-throat" exercise which does more to drive people away from Christ than to draw them to him. I call this exercise *exhibitionism*.

Jesus went to great lengths to expose exhibitionism in the Sermon on the Mount. He took the three main witnessing methods of the contemporary religion—almsgiving, prayer, and fasting—and he told the people to become incognito with all three!

What a stir he must have caused! When a devout believer of that day wanted to exhibit his faith, he did so by making a great show of giving his money, praying in public, and exhibiting a starvation syndrome. Now Jesus is saying, hide all three, because these so-called virtues are in fact *deadly virtues!* They are deadly because in the end they do not show God, they only *show off* the person who is trying to show God.

This is the clue to the difference between authentic witnessing and exhibitionism: the witness points to Christ; the exhibitionist points to himself. It's like comparing a ballerina with a stripper. We think of the ballerina as an artist and the stripper as an exhibitionist (at least, some of us do).

Why is the ballerina an artist and the stripper an exhibitionist? Aren't both dressed (undressed?) similarly? Don't both of them coordinate music with body movement?

The difference is that the ballerina uses her body and movements to point to a reality beyond herself—to a universal form. Her dance is a witness to a form and beauty (it *is* a form and a beauty) in which we can all participate.

The stripper, however, uses her dance to point precisely to herself. Her aim is to get the audience to want *her,* not something beyond her.

A witness uses his power to point to a reality (Jesus Christ) beyond himself, yet a reality of which he is a part. An exhibitionist uses the reality (Jesus Christ) to point to himself, i.e., to show off his own power. It was this basic shift in emphasis that led Jesus to tell his contemporaries to privatize their piety. Almsgiving, prayer, and fasting were meant to be symbols for pointing to God, but they had become means of merely pointing to the alms-givers, the pray-ers and the fast-ers.

Exhibitionism is deadly because it is subtle. A Christian can begin with a sincere desire to point people to God and end up only pointing to himself. The question is: how can we tell when this shift has occurred? How can we tell when we have stopped pointing to Christ and started pointing to ourselves? What are the telltale signs of exhibitionism?

For one thing, an exhibitionist seems more intent on selling Christ than sharing Christ. To share means to give to another what I myself have received. I did not create it; therefore I cannot change it, or reduce it, or package it. I can only give it in the same form as it was given to me.

Therefore, sharing Christ means sharing my own experience with Christ. As the old adage goes: "Every Christian has but one story to tell—the story of how God has dealt with him."

Sharing Christ also means that I must identify myself as a brother to the person with whom I'm sharing. I cannot *share* with one whom I regard as an alien. Someone has said that witnessing is not a case where one who is rich in righteousness dispenses it to someone who is poor in righteousness; *witness-*

*ing is one beggar telling another beggar where he has found
bread.*

However, *selling Christ* is something else. Instead of telling
his own story, the exhibitionist develops a spiel, a sales pitch,
replete with all the nuances of guilt and all the psychological
pressures of Madison Avenue. In fact, he can even sell Christ
without ever having experienced Christ himself!

For the exhibitionist, everything rests upon his sales record.
If he sells, he is a success, a "good company man." If he
doesn't sell, he is in trouble. Indeed, some churches and de-
nominations have their versions of the million-dollar round
table, by which the best salesmen are honored. Their pictures
are posted in the appropriate publications along with their
sales records. They lead seminars and training schools. Some
even get promoted to the executive echelon, where they no
longer have to sell at all. They only have to administer the
sales department!

Obviously, the selling approach to witnessing places the
emphasis upon the number of products sold and upon the
salesman, not upon the product itself. That's why exhibitionism is deadly. It replaces Christ with hyped-up sales promo-
tions.

Another result of the "selling Christ" approach is that it
tends to make the "salesman" dishonest. I discovered this dis-
honesty early in my ministry. I was pastoring a small church
in the countryside and commuting by car pool to the seminary.
My traveling companions were also student pastors who served
small churches in the area.

When we traveled to school every Tuesday, we would com-
pare our weekend successes. It was easy to tell who had had a
high attendance or a great number of conversions, because he
would be the first to ask, "How many did you guys have in
church Sunday? Did anybody get saved?"

I soon found that I was commuting with three highly successful evangelists, because every week they had higher attendances and more conversions to report!

My church was three miles from a paved road, had two outdoor privies, and forty members, all of whom (including the privies) were past middle-age. There weren't but sixty-five people in the whole community. Of the twenty-five non-Baptists, six were bedridden and seventeen were Methodists. That left me with only two bona fide sinners!

I didn't have much to brag about on Tuesdays. I worked hard to sell Christ to those two, but they had a head start on me. The pastors who preceded me had already practiced on them. They knew more "soul-winning" techniques than I did!

One Tuesday as I listened to my colleagues report their successes, I could stand it no longer. I related the most tear-jerking, cock-and-bull story imaginable, about how I had won a calloused farmer to Jesus. The preachers all said, "Praise the Lord." They also conveyed to me in nonverbal ways that I was now a certified member of the club.

By the end of the semester, I was "converting" as many as they were! The guilt I felt from those fabrications bothered me for a time, but their acceptance by my fellow pastors made up for it. Why, they even invited me to lead revival meetings in their churches.

I have thought about my car-pool deceptions over the years, both with a degree of guilt and amusement. It never occurred to me at the time that the number of conversions reported by my friends exceeded the entire population of the communities they served!

We were all playing the same game. We were being exhibitionists. We were gauging our self-worth by how many "policies" we were selling; and since there was a shortage of buyers, we made up some!

There is another telltale sign of the deadly virtue we're calling exhibitionism: *the exhibitionist is more concerned with being holy than he is with being loving.*

Langdon Gilkey brilliantly describes what I'm trying to say in his book *Shantung Compound*. When the Japanese overran China in World War II, they imprisoned all of the Caucasian aliens in a compound at Shantung. Persons from every walk of life were interned in a small area with little food and little living space. There were mining executives, laborers, professors, prostitutes, missionaries, drug peddlers, drug addicts, seamen, and vacationers.

In order to survive, the internees had to forge out an ordered society. Wealth, power, education, and all the criteria that order a regular society meant nothing.

At one point in his book, Gilkey comments on the effectiveness of the missionaries to heal the tensions in the camp and to produce a sense of community. With few exceptions, it was the nuns and priests who did the most to create brotherhood. Many of the Protestant missionaries, however, became responsible for the singlemost cause of strife and fragmentation!

Gilkey says that the reason behind the negative influence of these Protestants was that their chief concern lay in not wanting to be tainted by the unsavory influences in the camp. "Instead of bringing love and service into the world through God's calling," says Gilkey, "the Protestant began to try to keep himself 'holy' in spite of the world. . . . He ended up by concentrating only on avoiding the vices which might prevent him from being respectable." [1]

The Achilles heel of the exhibitionist is his contradictory desire to win people, but at the same time, to remain aloof from them. Gilkey's Protestants created fragmentation in the camp by regarding others as a threat to their holiness. Their strategy was to begin with a pitch to the nonbelievers which said, "You are not o.k., but I am o.k. . . . And if you want to be o.k. like I am, you must ape my lifestyle."

I should now like to say something positive about sharing Jesus Christ with those who do not know him. First, let me say that witnessing is done both verbally and nonverbally, that is, with words *and* deeds. It is really a waste of energy to debate whether witnessing is primarily a speaking exercise or an acting exercise; it is both. One without the other is a one-legged witness; it has no balance and makes no sense.

However, in most cases the right to verbalize our faith in Christ must first be earned by our showing a genuine love for the person to whom we are witnessing. Actions must precede words, if a trust-level is to be established. That's simply another way of saying that sharing Christ does not mean using a canned formula to confront strangers with whom we are unwilling to get involved. It must be an effort that comes out of one's total being.

Furthermore, sharing Christ must be a natural, almost effortless exercise. If a person has to change character and assume a stage face in order to share his faith, he is phony and his witness is phony. I cannot accept the view that reduces evangelism to mouthing a well-rehearsed spiel and seeks to train witnesses to change roles as the situation demands—a spiel for Moslems, a spiel for the rich, a spiel for the atheist, etc.

One of the best examples of witnessing I've run across is the statement made by D. M. Stanley after he had found David Livingstone in Africa (the famous "Dr. Livingstone, I presume" story). "I had no doubt that he [Livingstone] was a man consumed and driven by the Spirit of Jesus Christ," said Stanley, "and although he never spoke a word of it to me, had I stayed with him longer, I would have been compelled to become a Christian."

Livingstone had done business with Christ. His total life-expression witnessed to that fact. I'm certain that in due time he would have verbalized his faith to Stanley, but first he had to show the uniqueness that Christ had brought to his life. And he did this effortlessly.

My favorite TV commercial is the airline ad that shows the stewardess on board the plane attending to the passengers. She is strictly "sexy-sophisticate"—no go-go dancer, but no prim librarian, either. She glides down the aisle, adjusting the pillow for a grandmother, fastening a child's seatbelt, and turning the head of a junior executive. She looks straight into the camera and says, "If you've got it, flaunt it."

What is the "it" she's talking about? If you're a grandmother, the "it" is the special attention the airline gives to senior citizens. If you're a parent, "it" is the security your child receives while in flight. If you're a virile American male, you know very well what the "it" is!

But keep in mind that the stewardess does not herself say what the "it" is. She communicates "it"—we get the message all right—but she doesn't have to preach "it" to us. *"It" is that indefinable, desirable something that will make us book passage on the airline the next time we have the need to travel.*

The real message of the commercial is: *If you've got it, you don't have to flaunt it!* I think of Christian witnessing that way. If a person possesses the power of Jesus Christ in his life, he or she will exude a special, indefinable magnetism that will serve as a prompter to others. That magnetism is a far cry from the exhibitionism displayed by the girl in New Orleans.

You don't have to flaunt the power Christ brings to your life; it will flaunt itself. Isn't that what Jesus was saying to the exhibitionists of his day?

Witnessing is sharing by both word and deed the Christ you have met and are meeting in your own experience. If you've got him, you don't need to flaunt him. He will flaunt himself. Witnessing is not something you do, it is something you are. God doesn't need "holy persons" to hawk his wares. He needs folk who become Christ to others.

5. Certitude

THE VIRTUE OF
SECONDHAND FAITH

All I want is to know Christ and to experience the power of his resurrection, to share in his sufferings and become like him in his death, in the hope that I myself will be raised from death to life.

I do not claim that I have already succeeded in this, or have already become perfect. I keep striving to win the prize for which Christ Jesus has already won me to himself. Of course, my brothers, I really do not think that I have already won it; the one thing I do, however, is to forget what is behind me and do my best to reach what is ahead. So I run straight toward the goal in order to win the prize, which is God's call through Christ Jesus to the life above.

Philippians 3:10–14, TEV

ITEM: In a prisoner-of-war camp on the River Kwai,
        Japanese guards discover that a shovel is missing.
        They suspect that one of the P.O.W.'s has sold it
        to the Thai's for a profit. They demand that the
        guilty party step forward or else all prisoners will
        be executed. A Scottish soldier steps forward and
        says, "I did it." He is promptly shot to death.
        When the tools are counted again at the tool shed,
        no shovel is missing.

ITEM: A young man named Elliott hears of a South
        American tribe which has never heard the gospel.
        He goes to share Christ and is immediately killed.
        Later, his widow follows his footsteps and con-
        verts the very man who murdered her husband.

ITEM: A beautiful twenty-two-year-old woman estab-
        lishes a Christian school in a New York ghetto.
        Her witness threatens a street gang. They attack
        her. Both legs are broken; a bottle is smashed in
        her face, disfiguring her for life. Six months later,

71

she is released from the hospital and resumes her work in the ghetto.

What motivates such acts of religious heroism? Vengeance we expect. Self-preservation we expect. But we do not expect the kind of radical love exhibited in these true stories.

Ultimately, there is only one explanation: these people were operating with an inner certainty of God's presence. In other words, they were *sure* that what they were doing with their lives was more important than retaliation and self-preservation.

No one can do what they did without an inner vision, an inner certainty that what one is staking one's life on is indeed true. When tragedy strikes; when one is attacked by one's enemies; when the forces of evil seem insurmountable—no person can respond in love, unless he possesses the certainty of God's support and ultimate victory over evil.

Tom Dooley was once asked how he overcame disappointments and setbacks caused by uncaring people. "I simply remind myself of who is really keeping score," he said. No Christian can keep on keeping on without the certainty that it is God who is really keeping score in this world.

Where does a Christian obtain this certainty? In the final analysis, he receives it from a firsthand encounter with the living God. His association with Christian friends, his study of the Bible, and hearing the testimonies of others—all of these outside resources help him in his growth. But, ultimately, he must encounter God for himself, firsthand and one-to-one. The outside resources reinforce his personal experience with God, but they cannot serve as substitutes for it.

Catherine Marshall had it right when she said that God has no grandchildren. God is not a grandfather, he is only a father. Every individual must be born directly of God. Jesus informed Nicodemus, "You must be born again." [1] The emphasis is on the "you." "*You*, Nicodemus—*you*, the great religious teacher—even *you*, must be born again; in order to receive the inner certainty of God's presence."

So, certainty is a virtue which no Christian can do without. When all of the layers of faith are peeled back, there must be a kernel of certainty which remains.

However, there is a subtle perversion of the virtue called certainty. This has always plagued the Church and is still common in modern times. I call it *certitude*. Certitude has many of the outward appearances of certainty, and, like all the deadly virtues, it stems from sincere motives.

But there are two key differences between certainty and certitude: (1) they differ in the way they are received, and, (2) they differ in the way they are retained.

Certainty is received from firsthand experience; certitude is received from secondhand experience. In other words, certitude is secondhand religion. It is the acceptance of and adherence to religious convictions that have not been verified by firsthand experience.

A friend and colleague enrolled in his first Christian ethics class at the seminary. He was lectured thoroughly on the anti-Christian aspects of racial segregation. The professor equipped him with biblical and rational refutations of all of the arguments being put forth by the so-called "Christian segregationists." Immediately, he became a civil rights crusader in the pulpit, and, immediately, he began to meet with resistance from his congregation. The situation became so tense it appeared that he might be forced to resign. To complicate matters, several black persons presented themselves to his church for membership.

The church voted to deny their requests to join. Prudently, he "softened" his crusade somewhat. Later, he had occasion to live with a black family for several weeks. During his stay he came to experience the situation of these people firsthand. The couple he lived with had all the everyday concerns for their children that white parents have—were they brushing their teeth regularly? were they keeping the right company? were they doing their homework? etc.

The daily indignities they were forced to bear were insidious. Some days they had to miss a meal because they were in the wrong part of town at lunchtime. When they planned each day, they had to schedule their toilet stops according to the proximity of bathrooms not marked "Whites Only."

After this experience, my friend was no longer a civil rights crusader with secondhand arguments received from the classroom. That is, he was no longer the debater of a cause that happened to be in vogue at the time. He was now convinced that racial segregation was an inhuman, insane cancer eating at the jugular vein of civilized humankind. His conviction was now based upon firsthand experience, that is, upon certainty, not certitude.

The effects were visibly different. The church soon opened its doors to all people. A revolution took place, not because of his powers of persuasion, but because of the inner spiritual power that resides in any person who receives his convictions firsthand, as over against secondhand.

Helmut Thielicke speaks of the dearth of genuine prophetic preaching in our time—the kind of preaching that actually changes men's minds and behavior. He attributes the absence of such preaching to the fact that too many preachers are preaching convictions they themselves have not incorporated into their own existence. "Anybody who wants to know whether a particular soft drink is really as good as the advertising man . . . says it is," notes Thielicke, "cannot simply believe the phonetically amplified recommendations, but must find out whether this man actually drinks this soft drink at home when he is not in public. Does the preacher himself drink what he hands out in the pulpit?" [2]

Then Thielicke adds, "Obviously, anything that has the dignity of a conviction requires something more than *regarding* it to be true." [3] Convictions that are received secondhand can only be *regarded* as true. They may sound rationally airtight, but they have no convincing power. "Convincing convictions" must be received from firsthand experience.

Certitude is the product of secondhand experience. Certainty is received from firsthand experience.

Certitude differs from certainty, also, in the way it is *kept*. The Christian who has received his convictions from firsthand experience keeps them by constantly feeding them with new data. New ideas don't frighten him because he sees all truth as coming from God. His God is not a system to be defended but a living mysterious reality to be "kept up with" as He moves through history.

Therefore, the firsthand Christian retains his certainty by constantly allowing his beliefs to be exposed and refined by what God is doing *now*. New ideas and changes in the landscape of history are not his enemies; they are seen as progressive unveilings of God's will and personality.

The secondhand Christian however, can keep his convictions only by keeping them unexposed to new data. His God is not alive and progressively revealing himself; his God is already fully revealed, certified, and incorporated into the system that was given to him by others! In a word, he can keep God only by keeping the system unscathed and unaltered.

Kierkegaard observed that our desire to retain the old and the established in religion is really a secret selfishness based upon the pleasure principle. "It is the very man whose one intention is to enjoy life, and make a brilliant worldly career, to whom it may be of the greatest importance that there should be no disturbances where religion is concerned. Once the 'spirit' begins to move, life becomes unsettled, and one cannot concentrate properly on making a career. That is why it is so important that it should be kept as it is, that religion should be taken over exactly as it was transmitted by the last generation, with at the most a few little modifications." [4]

Thus, certainty comes from firsthand encounter with God

and is kept by repeated encounters with God. Certitude comes from blind acceptance of a body of religious propositions, and is kept by defending that body against change.

Some people believe that certitude is a trait found among religious conservatives only. This is not true. Certitude is very much at home with the liberals, too. You see, the liberal and the conservative are really brothers under the skin. *They are both intent on robbing God of the element of mystery.*[5] They both have God figured out and patented within a system.

The conservative has a system of doctrines, and he uses verses plucked from the Bible here and there to prove his doctrines. The Bible becomes a sort of "paper Pope." The liberal also has a system of doctrines, but he uses rational arguments instead of proof-texts in order to prove his system.

Both are alike in that they have prescribed boundaries for God's will, and they cannot allow the intrusion of any idea that contradicts their prescriptions. Perhaps this underlying similarity between the liberal and the conservative explains why it is that about all they can do is call each other names! They are alike in philosophical perspective, yet reach different conclusions, which means they find it difficult ever to teach each other.

This leads us to consider one of the deadly aspects of certitude. It cannot tolerate any serious dialogue between Christians who hold different opinions. Certitude demands that all Christians be *twin brothers* or not brothers at all!

I cannot believe that God would have the Christian world as fragmented as it is. "A house divided against itself cannot stand"—Jesus said that.

Last Christmas, I took my small son to the local shopping center to see Santa Claus. We waited in line for an hour. There were black, brown, white, and yellow children, all huddled together waiting to see Santa. No doubt there were also Baptists, Methodists, Catholics, and Presbyterians. The thought occurred to me: we can sit together at Santa's feet during the Christmas season, but we cannot sit together at the feet of the One whose birth we are celebrating.

Certitude is a deadly virtue because it divides the house of Christ against itself. That's not its only deadly aspect, however. Certitude has other lethal effects.

For example, the Christian who has received his convictions secondhand has to survive by isolating himself from the very world God is trying to save. If he steps outside his insular environment, he is lost. Again hear Kierkegaard:

> It is the tolerance of the orthodox which best shows how completely Christianity is lost. Their solution is: if only we may keep our religion to ourselves, the world can take care of itself. Merciful God, and that is supposed to be Christianity! . . . and so they come to an agreement; they wrap themselves up in their donkey-skin only asking that they be Christian themselves.[6]

As a minister near a university campus, I see this process of insulation frequently. A student will come to school from his hometown world of well-defined religious convictions. All his life he has accepted the "religion of the fathers" because it was simply *there* and because everybody else accepted it. Religious practice has been like hygienic practice. Going to church, bathing, shaving one's face, dousing oneself with deodorant are practices he accepted without ever questioning whether there was any good reason behind them.

Suddenly, the student finds himself in a new world—a world where no one particularly cares whether he obeys the religion of his fathers. Furthermore, he is offered all kinds of options to the religious convictions he has held. He discovers that his religion is of little value to him, now that he is no longer in his former environment. He is like a fish out of water.

A freshman coed enrolled in the university near our church and became active in our fellowship. She had been reared in a small town that was heavily influenced by the church. All extracurricular school programs and social functions were held in compliance with church activities and ethical biases. Consequently, on Sunday evenings the only "shows in town" for young people were either the Methodist Youth Fellowship (MYF) or the Baptist Training Union (BTU).

After she had been at the university for a few months, I asked how her religious upbringing had prepared her for coping with her new environment. "I've learned two things," she said. "First, there are a lot of happy pagans in this world. I was always told that people who had no religious moorings and who 'raised hell' all the time, were really miserable, riddled with neuroses, and begging desperately for the Christian gospel. This guy I've been dating is begging me for something, but, I can tell you, preacher, it's not the gospel he's begging for! In many ways, he's happier than I am!"

She went on: "The second thing I've learned is that if the kids in our town ever spent one Sunday night at Billy Joe's Discotheque, they'd never go to MYF or BTU again!"

The tragic truth is that many young people are spoon-fed a religion that cannot survive when it is exposed to the outside world. In short, their religion is an acculturated one.

I receive numerous letters from broken-hearted parents (often ordained ministers) pleading with me to contact their children who have "left the faith." They are haunted by the question, "What did I do wrong?"

The answer is, they probably didn't *do* anything wrong— not *willfully* at any rate. In their zeal to instill moral convictions in their children, they have imposed their own convictions upon them. But they have not led the children through the process of personal verification of these convictions. In short, the parents have given the children convictions without the tools of verification.

Quite often the reason this happens is that the parents themselves have not verified their own convictions. They blindly accepted them from their own parents and never worked through the sense of them. That process was easier in a former time because the whole culture pretty much agreed on what was right and wrong. The world was not fragmented as it is now. When a youngster went off to college, he was not leaving one environment for another. Today, things are different.

The result of the fragmentation of our culture is that young people are experiencing religious culture shock when they go to college. They are having the props knocked away from all those convictions they have blindly accepted. Many withstand the onslaught splendidly and verify their faith.

Others do not fare so well. They simply jump out of one cocoon into another. Some become chronic protesters. Posing as free-thinkers, they are not free at all. A free-thinker is someone who looks at all the evidence and then formulates his own view. The campus radicals I have known do nothing of the sort. Their position is always determined by the position of those with whom they disagree. They allow the opposition to determine their stance on every issue! As someone said, "The so-called campus liberal is liberal with everything but the other fellow's opinion."

So, some students who have been raised on a religion of certitude become slaves to protest. Others, however, find exotic cults and isms to replace the authoritarian cocoon they have rejected. I am convinced that the current infatuation of youth with Eastern mysticism (Hare Krishna, Yoga, transcendental meditation, et al) is simply the filling of a vacuum created by a Christian approach that has ignored the importance of one-to-one mystical encounter with God!

People who have received religion secondhand also tend to become desperate in a world of change like ours. When everything seems out of control, they cry for simple answers and authoritarian pronouncements. They rally to any figure who claims to have all the answers. This authoritarian figure tends to become their surrogate, their substitute, for a personal relationship with God.

The followers of the now infamous Rev. Jim Jones were such people. They were desperate. They felt bruised and abused by their society. Jones offered them "God in the flesh." Mix these ingredients with the isolation of the Guyanese jungle and Jones's paranoid tendencies and you have a tragic concoction. And, although Jonestown is an example of the most *extreme* results of secondhand faith, there are still a host of similarly desperate people who seem ready to give their lives and fortunes to anyone who claims to have "a direct line to God."

I could summarize the deadly effects of certitude by saying simply that certitude isolates Christians from Christians and Christians from the world. I should like to add a final word: Certitude also isolates the Christian from his God.

How does this isolation occur? I alluded to the answer earlier when I was marking the difference between certitude and certainty. Certitude demands a frozen God. In a world of constant change, it is humanly natural to seek something which is permanent, something that can withstand transience. When everything nailed down is coming loose, we want something to stay nailed down. Our tendency is to ascribe this permanence to God. We want a God we can locate at all times —a God who has said all he's going to say and done all he's going to do. We want to build a shrine, put him in it, and place security guards on the perimeters. We want a God like that of the girl who said, "Well, Jesus may have been a Jew, but God's a Baptist!"; or a God like that of the little boy who was sketching a picture in Sunday school and was asked by his teacher, "What are you drawing?" "I'm drawing a picture of God," he replied. "Oh, Johnny," said the teacher, "no one has ever seen God!" "Well, stick around," said he. "You will in a minute!"

Certitude demands a God who is entirely seeable, knowable, and predictable. In order to accomplish this goal, it must lock him within an immutable system. Whenever such an attempt is made, God becomes inaccessible. Here is a paradox: those who would seek God by reducing him and freezing him accomplish the precise opposite of their goal. In the Old Testament history, the Israelites repeatedly discovered that God's presence left them every time they tried to anchor him to a place or a thing. After all, idolatry is nothing more than an attempt to localize God within an image or a system.

The biblical God is a dynamic God. He is involved in history and moving it toward an ultimate goal. God's nature and his intentions for the world have been shown to us in the person of Jesus Christ. God intends to remake the world into Christ's image, where God and man are one in a free and personal relationship. If we want to know what God is like and what he intends for men ultimately to be like, look at Jesus; he is the model.

The Christian's task is to get with God's program, to become his partner in the plan—to penetrate the world, not to withdraw from it. This is possible only through a firsthand relationship with God.

Certitude attempts to anchor God to one place and time, and it encourages us to withdraw from the world.

Someone said that living the Christian life is like riding a bicycle; you're either on or you're off. There can be no stopping, or you're dead. Certainty is the virtue of "bicycle faith." It's the kind of faith in which the believer knows God from firsthand experience and yet also knows that there is more to know; so he keeps moving and discovering.

Certitude is the virtue of "tricycle religion"—the kind that wants to rest in one place without falling. It cannot be done.

I think this was Paul's message in the Scripture printed at the first of this chapter. He tells his Philippian friends that he has not reached a stopping place in his pilgrimage with God, *because there is no such thing as a stopping place.* "All I want is to know Christ," he says, "to become like him. . . . I do not claim that I have already succeeded in this. . . . I run straight toward the goal in order to win the prize, which is God's call through Christ Jesus to the life above."

Paul had certainty. He knew God firsthand. He had met him face to face one day on a dusty road. But Paul did not have *certitude*—a neatly packaged, reductionistic system. He knew that he had miles to go before he slept.

6. Velvet Violence

THE VIRTUE OF
THE RIGHTEOUSLY INDIGNANT

"You have heard that it was said: 'An eye for an eye and a tooth for a tooth.' But now I tell you: do not take revenge on someone who wrongs you. If anyone slaps you on the right cheek, let him slap your left cheek too. And if someone takes you to court to sue you for your shirt, let him have your coat as well. . . .

"You have heard that it was said: 'Love your friends, hate your enemies.' But now I tell you: love your enemies, and pray for those who persecute you, so that you may become the sons of your Father in heaven."

Matthew 5:38–40, 43–45a, TEV

"VIOLENCE IS AS American as apple pie." I think H. Rap Brown, the militant black radical, said that. Most Americans didn't like it. Maybe it was because the guy who said it was rather violent himself. But perhaps that wasn't the only reason. Some accusations have a way of striking us in the quick . . . they are too true to tolerate.

I suspect that is the case with Mr. Brown's statement, for the history of America is a violent one. Violence has become an efficient tool for solving complex problems.

We established the Republic by violent revolution; the Indian problem was "solved" by violent methods; the war with Japan was shortened by the introduction of nuclear holocaust; and America has repeatedly attempted to establish democracy in foreign lands by violent means.

The examples above, plus the fact that movie and television producers cannot sell their wares without airing violence-oriented subject matter, lead one to the conclusion that we are indeed a violent people.

The American penchant for violence has not bypassed the religious spectrum. Violence is alive and well in the American Christian community. However, Christian violence is what I call "velvet violence." It has a soft, almost innocent appearance. It is not the blood-and-guts variety, yet it is every bit as destructive to the human spirit.

I first discovered velvet violence as a young preacher. I was leading a revival meeting at a smalltown church in southern Texas. I had no more then five sermons, and they were borrowed.

On the last evening of the meeting, when I had finished my meager remarks, the pastor of the church came forward and faced the congregation. He began to weep. "We all know that this young preacher has a lot to learn," he said, nodding toward me. "But I want to tell you, being with him this week and observing his zeal and hope has given me a new vision. I have grown stale over the years. I haven't liked myself and I haven't liked most of you. I've been doing my job strictly as a means of supporting my family and because I don't know how to do anything else."

He went on. "Tonight I would like to make a new start. I want to be a better pastor, and I hope you will give me the chance." He sat down.

For a moment, there was silence. Then a man stood. "That was a touching speech," he said, "and I know that Brother Fred means to do better. But I think it's too late. He's been here ten years and he's done very little. Frankly, I think we'd all be better off if he moved on."

The people nodded solemnly. Two weeks later the preacher was gone. I asked some of those people if the pastor had ever made such a public confession before and learned that he had not.

That was velvet violence! Those people destroyed that preacher as efficiently as if they had put a gun to his head. No doubt he had been derelict in his duties. Perhaps he had been so derelict that he needed to be fired. But the *way* it was done is what I wish to emphasize. The tone of vengeance, the intent to hurt and maim, the cruelty—*all were employed un-*

der the guise of righteous indignation. Those people convinced themselves that they were justified on godly grounds to destroy a man's career.

Righteous indignation is always the front for the covert operations of velvet violence. It's the justification we use to clean up violence and make it look respectable. It's the vehicle by which violence comes to be regarded as a Christian virtue.

There is a *legitimate* righteous indignation. I am not advocating that we should not be angered by the injustices of this world; nor am I urging that we should sit idly by and allow them to flourish. Jesus certainly didn't. He drove out the money-changers, and with a whip, too!

However, there is a point at which the righteously indignant become more intent upon punishing offenders than upon eradicating injustices. It is at this point that righteous indignation becomes a masquerade for violence.

Whenever a Christian sets out on a crusade to eradicate evil, it would be good for him to ask himself what he really wants. Does he want to rid the world of the evil itself, or does he want to hurt the offender? If the offender is the target, then righteous indignation has become velvet violence.

I sometimes suspect that some moral crusaders would rather that evil not be cured at all, if it meant that the people who did the evil would not be punished. These crusaders cannot be satisfied unless somebody is flogged, racked, and bruised. There are some who would be grossly disappointed if God were to let everybody off scot-free at the Judgment Day! They operate on the assumption that evil cannot be cured unless somebody gets it in the neck!

The tragedy is that this love of blood is actually seen in some quarters as a Christian virtue! It is believed that the world is divided into two classes—the good guys and the bad guys—and that the good guys are quite justified in using violence to do away with the bad guys. In fact, they are often applauded for their efforts.

One does not have to consider for very long what Jesus said about violence in order to see how deadly this perversion of righteous indignation can be. If I use evil in order to combat evil men, I have not gotten rid of the evil . . . I have only perhaps gotten rid of the evildoers! Also I have increased the number of evil's allies in the world by becoming one of them myself.

Isn't this the point Jesus was making with the "eye-for-an-eye" analogy? He was saying, "Let's suppose that you strike me and put out my eye. And let's say your deed provokes me to respond in like fashion. You knocked out my eye, so I knock out yours. My action only provokes you to knock out my other eye. Then, of course, I extinguish your remaining eye. What is the result? We're both blind, we've both used evil tactics, and the only thing remaining strong is the evil itself!"

Have I put words into Jesus' mouth? I don't think so. His logic was very elementary: using evil to combat evil simply causes evil to proliferate. He not only said that, he also lived it. He refused to respond in kind to those who did evil to him.

As elementary as this sounds, we continue to practice the insidious eye-for-an-eye philosophy. And we practice it in the Church as well as in the other arenas of life.

Velvet violence also saps the creative energy of God's people. People who are out to get evildoers have a way of being consumed by their mission.

A current trend in the world of news reporting illustrates how honest crusades against evil can become all-consuming crusades against *individual persons*. In the aftermath of the Vietnam War and Watergate, it has become an unwritten law that the surest way for a journalist to establish his reputation is to *get somebody*.

I realize that it is difficult to separate evil from those who commit evil, but I also think it is safe to say that there was a time when the journalistic world was more interested in eradicating wrongs of society than it was in attacking notable persons. Ours is a celebrity-oriented society. Big people are big news; and big news is big business. Therefore, nothing sells newspapers and boosts TV ratings like the exposure of the private lives and morals of public figures.

However, we must not be too hard on the press. It caters to the public's taste. Seamy scandals are what we crave, and they are what we are fed in a steady diet. The answer is not to muzzle the press but to muzzle ourselves! Too many of us prefer attacking evildoers to eradicating evils, and this lustful preference consumes us. It blurs our vision of the whole and saps our creative energy.

Translated into Christian terms, the point is this: we can serve the purposes of God best by concentrating upon how to change evildoers. I like what Lincoln said when one of his advisers urged him to get rid of a political enemy by attacking him. There are two ways to dispose of an enemy, he said, either by destroying him or by making him a friend. Lincoln chose to make the man a friend.[1]

Up to this point, I have emphasized two deadly effects of the perversion of righteous indignation which I call velvet violence: (1) it proliferates evil instead of eradicating it, and (2) it consumes the creative energy of God's people. There is another deadly aspect of velvet violence which we need to consider. When it is elevated to the status of a virtue, it completely blocks out the method Jesus used to combat evil.

Earlier, I mentioned Jesus' approach briefly. Now I should like to look at it in detail. Simply stated, Jesus dealt with evil by responding to it in contrast. He refused to play the game by the opponent's rules. He returned good for evil, peace for violence, love for hatred. He did not strengthen evil by adding to it. He did not give his opponent fresh provocation by returning a slap for a slap.

I believe Jesus chose this route because he was convinced that every person had the capacity to act nobly if the vicious cycle of violence to which he was accustomed could be broken. The most violent person could be prompted to act peaceably if he could encounter an adversary who refused to respond to his violence with violence. In short, Jesus believed that the only way to cure a violent nature was to show it an alternative!

Obviously, Jesus' approach is risky. Eventually it cost him his life at the hands of violent men. It would be easy to believe that Jesus was a dreamy idealist who didn't really "know the score."

All sorts of questions arise when one attempts to put Jesus' approach to violence into practice. For instance, how could we use Jesus' method in international relations? Should we refuse to respond to a Hitler by taking up arms? Should we have allowed the Third Reich to consume the world without resistance?

What about bullies? If one refuses to stand up to a bully, he leads the bully to think that he is weak and only encourages the bully to increase his tyranny. Should we allow bullies to go unchallenged?

Consider the slum lords. Should we refuse to crush their tyranny? Should we pat them on the head and send them a new batch of poor people to exploit?

And what about criminals? Should we close all the prisons and set the inmates free to prey upon the innocent?

A multitude of questions challenge the validity of Jesus' response-in-contrast method for eradicating evil. In all honesty I cannot give airtight answers to all of them. Perhaps we should regard bullies, whether they be individuals or nations, as sick persons who have to be separated by force if necessary from normal society. Perhaps slum lords are like the money-changers in the Temple—they must be deprived of the right to prey upon the weak.

Criminals have to be forcibly detained for their own good, as well as for the sake of public order and the protection of the innocent.

In a word, we do not live in an ideal world. However, before we reject Jesus' method we should consider several things. First, what is the alternative? This world where violence reigns supreme is the kind of world we have at present. Forgiveness and peace are, at best, myths. We've been trying the violent method for centuries, and it hasn't brought us very far beyond the cave!

Another thing to consider is the motives that lie behind our treatment of the Hitlers, the bullies, the slum lords, and the criminals. Why do we have armies and prisons? To punish evildoers, or to rehabilitate them?

We must also ask ourselves these questions: Shall we sacrifice a humanity which thrives on peace and understanding for a subhumanity which thrives on violence? Is it better to live in a violent world as a violent person, or is it better to die trying to promote peace?

I read of a woman who saw a dog stranded on some floating debris in an icy river. She risked her own life and rescued the animal; but it bit her and she died of rabies.[2] We must make a basic choice: shall we dare to risk our own security by trying Jesus' method for rescuing a violent world, or shall we let it be swept away to destruction?

Jesus' formula for dealing with evil may sound idealistic and risky; but I believe it is the only option we have. As a first step we might at least try Jesus' method for responding to violence on a personal basis. I have found that it works amazingly well. I met recently with a group of ministers at a luncheon to hear a fellow-minister propose a mission project to the local university.

The minister was zealous and sincere in his burden for the spiritual welfare of the university community. He needed funds from our churches in order to accomplish his goal. The luncheon was the occasion for him to sell us his ideas and to raise $25,000.

We were seated at a table in a large restaurant. The minister was outlining his program with enthusiasm. A waitress came over and politely asked if he might turn down the volume a bit, since he was disturbing the customers. For a few minutes, he was more subdued, but soon he was shouting again.

Suddenly, a huge, hairy, rough-looking man walked up to the table and said to us, "That's the biggest *;#?! I ever heard! I'm sitting over there trying to enjoy a few drinks, and you holy-Joes keep shouting all this *#!?! about Jesus. If you ever had one snort of cocaine, you'd never mention Jesus again!"

"God have mercy on you, brother," said the minister. "Some day you will bow before Jesus and wish you hadn't said that."

The argument continued and got more heated. The hairy fellow would curse and the preacher would threaten him with eternal damnation.

It occurred to me that the preacher was playing the same game as the ruffian. Seemingly he was unaware that he was returning violence for violence. Violence was gaining complete control of the situation. I wondered how it would end. I feared the worst . . . the hairy fellow had his fists clenched for combat.

About that time one of my fellow-preachers stood, walked around the table, and faced the man. "Sir," he said, "I am sorry that we disturbed you. I would count it a privilege if you would allow me to pay for your drinks." The man was stunned. (So were the preachers.) The preacher reached over and took the check from his hand. The man stood there, undecided and awkward for a moment, and then left, chuckling nervously.

Response-in-contrast—it worked! The man was not converted—he probably resumed life as usual—but I doubt that he will soon forget that moment. Most of all, the violence of that situation was defused before it could explode.

The minister who had come to sell us his program was obviously threatened by this incident. He said to the peacemaker, "You just did something I would never do. You paid for alcohol, and you led that man to think we are cowards." The peacemaker said nothing, but the rest of us pitched in to help him pay the man's bar tab!

The tragic thing about this incident is that the visiting preacher never seemed to realize that his righteous indignation bore all the marks of velvet violence. The man had attacked him and he was responding in kind. His dissatisfaction with our colleague seemed in reality to be a dissatisfaction over not having been able to return his opponent's blows in full measure. He was apparently convinced that the ruffian was an alien, an enemy, and that we were the "good guys."

Jesus did not divide people into such neat categories. The seeds of violence, whether the velvet kind or the bloody variety, are planted whenever we begin to separate people into the categories of "we" and "they." Once we look at others as "other," we are prime candidates for violence. An Arab legend tells of a Bedouin in the desert. In the distance he sees an image approaching. "It is only a mirage," he says. But the figure gets larger as it comes toward him. "No, it is a monster!" he says. Then, as the figure begins to take definite shape, the Bedouin raises his sword in fear. "No," he says, it is my enemy." But, when they come face to face, he says, "Ah, it is only my brother!"

Velvet violence begins the moment we regard others as aliens. It proliferates when we become intent upon eradicating evildoers rather than evil. And it blocks our way to Jesus' method of responding to evil. Yet, some of us persist in calling it a virtue.

7. Independence

THE VIRTUE OF
THE IRRESPONSIBLE

Then Jesus told this story to some who boasted of their virtue and scorned everyone else:

"Two men went to the Temple to pray. One was a proud, self-righteous Pharisee, and the other a cheating tax-collector. The proud Pharisee 'prayed' this prayer: 'Thank God, I am not a sinner like everyone else, especially like that tax collector over there! For I never cheat, I don't commit adultery, I go without food twice a week, and give to God a tenth of everything I earn.'

"But the corrupt tax collector stood at a distance and dared not even lift his eyes to heaven as he prayed, but beat upon his chest in sorrow, exclaiming, 'God, be merciful to me, a sinner!' I tell you, this sinner, not the Pharisee, returned home forgiven! For the proud shall be humbled, but the humble shall be honored."

Luke 18:9–14, *Living Bible*

OF ALL THE contributions Jesus made to the world, among the greatest was the belief in the *worth of the individual*. His every word and deed were governed by his love for the singular person. He came to save the whole world, but he saw the whole in terms of the one. Verify this by noting how many times Jesus turned away from a crowd to minister to the needs of one person: Zacchaeus; the woman with an incurable hemorrhage; the demoniac; the woman at the well in Samaria; the cripple at the pool of Bethesda; the rich young ruler; the woman caught in adultery; the blind man, Bartimaeus; and the son of a Roman officer.

Whenever we see Jesus ministering to people, we see him caring for individuals. Any system, power, or law that sought to rob the freedom of the individual Jesus was quick to call "demonic." The *real* reason he threatened the religious and political establishments of his day was that he affirmed the worth of the "little guy."

In a moving passage from *Dr. Zhivago,* the Russian author Boris Pasternak says:

Rome was a flea market of borrowed gods and conquered peoples, a bargain basement on two floors, earth and heaven, a mass of filth convoluted in a triple knot as in an intestinal obstruction. Dacians, Heruleans, Scythians, Samaritans, Hyperboreans, heavy wheels without spokes, eyes sunk in fat, sodomy, double chins, illiterate emperors, fish fed on the flesh of learned slaves. There were more people in the world than there have been ever since, all crammed into the passages of the coliseum and all wretched. And into this tasteless heap of gold and marble, He came, light and clothed in an aura, emphatically human, deliberately provincial, Galilean; And at that moment gods and nations ceased to be and man came into being, man the carpenter, man the plowman, man the shepherd with his flock of sheep at sunset, man who does not sound in the least proud, man thankfully celebrated in all the cradle songs of mothers and in all the picture galleries the world over.[1]

No wonder the Soviet government suppressed the publication of these the words of one of her own sons; for they strike at the heart of Soviet atheism. *Strictly* speaking, the Soviet Union should not be called an atheistic nation simply because it officially denies belief in the God of Christendom. It should be called atheistic because it denies what the Christian God stands for, namely, the worth of the individual.

On the other hand, if there is any sense in which America could be called a "Christian nation," it is not because most of its people claim affiliation with Christian churches. America is "Christian" only in so far as she too preserves the worth of the individual.

Harry Emerson Fosdick said in his autobiography that his lifelong endeavors to relate the Christian faith to everyday life were governed by one central conviction—"that the ultimate criterion of any civilization's success or failure is to be found in what happens to the underdog." [2] Then he quotes Lord Asquith's test for determining whether a nation is Christian. "The test," said Asquith, "is the point below which the weakest and most unfortunate are allowed to fall." [3]

Whether a nation is Christian or un-Christian should *not be determined* by its official religious pronouncements, *but by the lengths to which it will go to guarantee the worth of persons.*

In a sense, it can be said that the one Christian virtue upon which all of the others rest is the worth of the individual. It is true that Jesus summed up all the demands of Christian living by telling us to love God with all our being. But then he added a qualifying phrase in order to show us how to carry out this love toward God. The way to love God is by *loving our neighbor as ourselves.* We love God by loving our neighbor, by treating him as a supreme object of worth. To love God and neighbor are one in the same.

Thus, the spirit of individualism is the supreme Christian virtue. Yet as is the case with all of the Christian virtues, individualism can become a deadly virtue. Remember the central thesis of this book: evil always attacks the Christian, not at his weak points, but at his strong. There is a deadly perversion of individualism which appears honorable and good and which is much admired in the world today. I call it *independence.*

The spirit of independence begins with all of the noble assumptions of the spirit of individualism. It says that every person has the inalienable right to think and choose for himself and that no power on earth can violate this right. But then it goes one fatal step beyond this position, and says, "Therefore, I'm free to behave as I like; I'm not responsible for the well-being of others; I'm absolutely autonomous and independent of the God who created me, of the world into which I was born, and of the human community in which I live."

In other words, the spirit of independence uses the insights of Christian individualism as an excuse for not being responsible for others! Individualism says, "Every human being is a creature of supreme value; therefore, I am responsible for what happens to every person." Independence says, "Every human being is a creature of supreme value; therefore, I as a creature of value am not responsible for anyone but myself. . . . I am independent of obligations to anyone!" Christian individualism is an every-man-for-others enterprise while independence is an every-man-for-himself enterprise.

Another way to distinguish individualism from independence is to address the question of how a person can best come to realize his uniqueness as a person. The spirit of Christian individualism answers that one is most uniquely himself when he is part of a community, when he is involved in helping others realize their own unique worth. The spirit of independence answers that one is most uniquely himself when he is isolated from community and doing his own thing, when he is possessed with a feeling of absolute sovereignty, and when the community's claims upon him are seen merely as concessions which he makes to insure his personal security.

I know a man who deals in exotic animals. His specialty is reptiles. He transports snakes, crocodiles, and lizards to zoos all over the world. I asked him how he kept the reptiles docile while in transit. "I keep them full," he said. "Before I ship them, I let them gorge themselves. They sleep through the whole trip." Such is the claim of the spirit of independence. It is based upon the belief that our hunger for happiness and our need for aggression can be satisfied by material goods and peaceful isolation. But Christian individualism sees that we are not made that way. We can glut ourselves with the material and still remain lonely, hostile creatures. Only communion with each other can fulfill our hunger.

Science has shown us that all of life is characterized by organization. There is no such thing as organic independence. Everything that exists depends upon something else. Life is a symphony, not a solo. We have learned that polluting one small part of the natural environment sets off a chain reaction that eventually comes full circle and pollutes our own bodies. The history of cultures also affirms the necessity of interdependence and the insanity of independence. Never has a civilization survived, once its people began to interpret individualism as a license to withdraw from caring for each other.

Yet modern society seems bent on ignoring the evidence. I can think of two examples that indicate this is true. The advent of big government is one. Government has come to be regarded as an enemy rather than a protector. It is seen as a watchman who keeps us looking over our shoulders. Everyone seems to be complaining about government's intrusion upon private life, but few seem to realize the reason for the intrusion.

I am convinced it has occurred as a direct result of the spirit of independence. When manufacturers started making inferior products at superior prices, the government stepped in. When people began denying other people their basic human rights, the government established a human rights police force. The government now regulates everything from banks to toilet paper, simply because the society took individualism to mean the right to get what one wants at the expense of others.

A second example of the deadliness of independence is contained in the phrase, "I don't want to get involved." I'll forego the dramatic illustrations and ask you to consider the frame of mind that lies behind that phrase. When a person says, "I don't want to get involved," he's claiming the right to ignore the needs of others. He's saying, "I am a free individual, which means, that while I am not free to hurt others, I am free *not* to help them if I so choose."

These are but two examples of the deadly effects of independence. There are many more, not only upon society in general but upon the Church in particular. With some churchmen in America, especially by those of Protestant persuasion, the same subtle shift from a belief in individualism to a spirit of independence has occurred.

The Protestant spirit began with the altogether legitimate

conviction that every believer must stand alone before God and must follow his own individual conscience as he is led by the Holy Spirit. He needs no intermediary between himself and God. "Only faith" and "only Scripture" are the authorities proclaimed by Reformation. In my denomination, this conviction is called "the priesthood of the believer," meaning that each believer is his own priest and can go directly to God for his marching orders.

Obviously, this emphasis upon individualism came as a reaction to totalitarian Christianity. The reaction has gone too far, however. Today, many Christians are of the opinion that they have no obligations to the Church as a *community*. They are proponents of what Ernest Campbell calls "religion a la carte".[4] They pick and choose only the parts of the menu that suit their liking; that is, what they will believe about God, what forms of devotion they will practice, what morals they will adhere to, and what parts of Christ's mission they will support.

Just as society in general is fragmented, so is the Church. There is little integrity to church membership. One doesn't have to be responsible in order to be a member in good standing. The Church is easier to join and harder to get kicked out of than most any other organization. Russell Bow points out: "Almost every other institution has standards or requires disciplines. The Church requires less of its members than is expected by a good luncheon club. When a patient goes to a hospital, he gets into bed and submits to some rather unpleasant hospital routines. But one can join the Church by simply having his name on the roll, and can remain a member for years without attending, paying, or submitting to any disciplines except those of his own choosing."[5]

The point is that when independence becomes a virtue, the church cannot be a community in the biblical sense. Paul's dominant analogy for describing the Church is the "body of Christ." The Church's nature is like the human anatomy. Each member has its *unique* contribution to make to the

body's function, that is, each member is of individual worth
and importance. But an individual member acting separately
not only deprives the body but also destroys itself. The individual's uniqueness can be realized only as he acts in concert
with the other parts.[6]

The discoveries of modern physiology have reduced the
human anatomy to smaller entities than Paul knew of, but
they have only confirmed that his "body" analogy for the
Church was a good one. We now know that the human body
is composed of cells and even smaller entities; but the truth
remains that although each cell has its own individuality, it
cannot operate separately without destroying the whole and
itself.

Cancer begins when a single cell goes awry and begins to
multiply on its own. What an analogy for the Church! The
Body of Christ is suffering from a malignancy these days—a
malignancy called independence. Many of the Body's "cells"
have decided to function independently. Instead of contribut-
ing to the Body's nourishment, they are consuming it an inch
at a time. And the tragedy is that the independent spirit of
these singular cells is seen by many as a virtue.

The true spirit of the church is the *spirit of fellowship*. It
recognizes that every person is a unique creation of God with
unique gifts. But it also recognizes that every person cannot
realize his uniqueness until he gives away his gifts within a
loving community. As Tournier puts it:

There are two ways to become oneself . . . There is the
negative way of revolt, contradiction, refusal to obey, and
complaining. This weakens the group and does nothing to
strengthen the person. Then there is the positive affirmation
of the self, which unwittingly comes from serving the larger
group.[7]

In a word, the New Testament formula for true individualism is service within community. In Jesus' words, "Let him

who would become great be a servant." [8] On the other hand, the spirit of independence is a revolt, not only against man but also against God. It refuses to acknowledge its reliance upon anyone outside itself.

And so we are back to the recurring reason why each of the Christian virtues becomes a deadly virtue—man would be a god unto himself. All the deadly virtues begin here. They all find their genesis in pride. That's why I introduced this chapter with Jesus' story of the Pharisee and the tax collector who went to the Temple to pray. The Pharisee is a deadly man, not because he is insincere, but precisely because he is sincere and is *proud* of it.

There is a well-worn saying that "the road to hell is paved with good intentions." We often think that the "good intentions" are the half-hearted efforts we easily discard. On the contrary, I think they are the ones we hold to so strongly that they become the occasions for an intense pride. The Pharisee had good intentions, and he was darn well proud of them, too! Any virtue + pride = a deadly virtue.

Afterthought

TOWARD AN ANTIDOTE
FOR THE DEADLY VIRTUES

My WIFE WAS THE first to read the manuscript of this book. (I hope she isn't the last.) That's the way I wanted it. She has always been my best critic, in spite of the fact that all husbands are expected to say things like that. To my anxious "Whataya think?" she promptly replied, "I think you have made a deadly virtue out of exposing deadly virtues." 'Nuff said.

It is one thing to diagnose an illness, but it is another to provide an antidote for its cure. Therefore, I should like to offer a supportive word to those pilgrims who are involved in the struggle to keep their Christian virtues from becoming deadly virtues.

What is the antidote for the deadly virtues? It is not a law or an action, it is a principle. It's a way of thinking that must pervade all rules and actions. Several years ago, Carlisle Marney gave me this principle without explaining it. He was running a "repair shop for broken preachers" in North Carolina. Ministers who were disillusioned and suffering from identity crises came to his Interpreter's House from all over the country.

I asked Marney what his experience had shown the most

important principles to be for a minister to learn in order to keep his emotional and spiritual balance. He said, "There are two: (1) A minister must learn how to say 'I'; and (2) he must learn the *real* difference between saints and sinners."

I understood immediately what he meant by the first principle. A minister without ego-strength—that is, without an awareness of his self-worth before God—is doomed. With arrows flying from every direction, a minister had better love himself and know that God loves him, if he expects to keep his balance.

It took some time, however, before I understood what Marney meant by "knowing the *real* difference between saints and sinners." As I said, he didn't explain his meaning, but I think he was pointing to one of the recurring principles of this book —namely, that sincere Christians become hypocrites the moment they begin to think of themselves as a separate human species; that is, the moment they begin to think that there is an essential difference between themselves and unbelievers. It is this feeling of exclusivism that corrupts our virtues and makes them deadly.

It was also this air of exclusivism that made the Pharisees the archenemies of Jesus. They eventually turned the tide of public opinion against him by charging him with blasphemy, but their *real quarrel* with him lay in the fact that he kept the company of sinners, outcasts, and tax-collectors. The Pharisees had neatly separated humanity into the categories of saints and sinners, and they could not tolerate Jesus' association with the latter.

Jesus answered their accusations by telling them in essence that they didn't have the foggiest notion of the *real* difference between saints and sinners. In order to expose their misconceptions, he told the three celebrated parables recorded in Luke 15.

"Suppose a shepherd has a hundred sheep and loses one," he says. "What does he do? He leaves the ninety-nine and searches for the one. When he finds it, he celebrates. And suppose a woman has ten coins and loses one of them. She searches until she finds it; then she calls in her friends to celebrate the coin's return."

Then Jesus tells a third parable which we know as the story of the Prodigal Son.

The point is that Jesus was giving an antidote for the exclusivism of the Pharisaical mind. The virtues of the Pharisees were deadly because they had misunderstood the difference between saints and sinners.

What was he saying through these parables?

One thing is obvious: *the difference between a saint and a sinner is not a moral difference.* A saint is not a saint because he's morally worth more than a sinner. The sheep who strayed from the flock didn't become lost because he was morally worse than the others. He simply "nibbled" himself lost. He put his head down, started grazing, and without noticing, he became separated from the fold.

Obviously, many people become separated from "God's fold" by doing likewise. They pursue what they consider to be worthy and harmless goals. Their straying is not intentional at the outset. They don't become lost because they are "worse" than others.

The lost coin was not a "bad" coin. It was lost because it was dropped by careless hands. The same can be said for persons. Many so-called sinners are not in God's "bag" because at some point in their lives they were dropped, abused by careless hands. Kenneth Chafin tells of the time he was a guest speaker at a church, and following his first sermon, a man came forward to profess his faith in Christ. The man had a questionable reputation in the community, and the people of the church were elated that he had seen the light.

The next day, Chafin and the local minister visited the man to talk further with him about his decision. The man greeted them exuberantly. He was bubbling over with happiness. He

ushered them in, asked that they be seated, and then, to celebrate his newly found faith, proceeded to serve them beer.

The pastor and his congregation were staunch teetotalers.
Beer-drinking was high on the priority list of "sins." Chafin
says that the minister immediately informed the man that there
was no way he could be considered one of the saints and drink
beer. Bewildered and angry, the man asked them to leave his
home and never to return. He was ready to accept Christ, but
not the list! The minister concluded that the man's decision
for Christ had not been genuine after all.

Many have been dropped by the careless hands of those
who would distinguish saints from sinners on the basis of a
"moral list." I have the honor of being the friend of a famous
country-western singer. He has the reputation of being godless
and proud of it. Nothing is further from the truth. He is a
gentle and loving man who never utters an unkind word about
others.

Recently he did a religious concert and rap session at our
church. The place was packed with young people. During our
dialogue, I asked him why a man with his understanding of
the Christian spirit never attended church. He said that years
ago he had been a Bible teacher at a local church. He was a
carpenter by trade, but he earned additional income by playing his guitar on Saturday evenings at a local tavern.

A group from his church called one day and informed him
that he would either have to stop picking his guitar in the
tavern or stop teaching the Bible-class. "They didn't censure
the electrician who wired the tavern, or the plumber who
plumbed it, or the kitchen supply man who sold the glasses,"
he said, "and they were all members of my church. But they
censured me for making a living off of the same place." Then
he added, "My relationship with God was no different then
than it is now; but this is the first time I've been inside a
church building for twenty years." When I asked why he had
consented to come, he said, "Well, this church seems to accept
people as people, and there's only one kind, you know."

The difference between saints and sinners is not a moral one. The lost sheep and the lost coin weren't lost because they were any worse or any better than the others. But what of the prodigal son in the third parable? He went to a far country and wasted himself *by choice,* didn't he? Yes, he did; but Jesus is careful to point out that, morally speaking, he was no worse than his brother who stayed at home and obeyed all the rules.

What Jesus was trying to show in these stories is that, when it comes to "good and bad," all people are *morally the same.* We may have different methods for sinning, but we all manage to sin quite adequately, one way or another.

The antidote for the deadly virtues is to constantly remember that the difference between saints and sinners is not a moral difference. When we understand this, there can be no occasion for seeing ourselves as a separate species. I'm fond of the story comedian David Steinberg tells of meeting a hippie on the street. The man was dirty and covered with hair. He wore beads and tattered clothing. He said to Steinberg, "Hey, man, do I know you, or do you just remind me of somebody?" "I probably remind you of God," said Steinberg. "After all, I was created in his image, you know. Come to think of it, you remind me somewhat of him yourself." Saints and sinners are all people created in the image of God, and the difference between people is not moral. The Pharisees didn't know this. They still don't.

What *is* the difference between saints and sinners, then? In a word, *a saint is at home with God and a sinner is not.* The only difference between the lost sheep and the ninety-nine was that the latter were in the shepherd's corral. They could hear his voice, receive his instructions, and be protected from their enemies. The lost sheep had none of these privileges. He was the easy victim of every predator. He was cut off from the gracious support of his master and from the care of his community. He had no potential for growth and survival.

The nine coins in the woman's purse were useful and pro-

ductive, "valuable." The lost coin, however, had no produc-
tive potential. It was useless, worthless.

The lost son was different from his older brother only
because he was not at home with the Father.

The lost sheep, the lost coin, and the lost son all had one
thing in common: they weren't "at home," so to speak, which
is simply another way of saying that they were cut off from
becoming what they could be. They weren't reaching their
potential. "To be at home with the Father" means to be in a
position to become what one can be, that is, to be capable of
reaching one's potential.

A saint is someone who has the power to be becoming. A
sinner is someone who does not have the power to become
what he was created to be. The difference between them is not
a matter of moral rectitude or worth; it is a matter of being in
a relationship to God that enables a person to use his gifts in
order to make the world in Christ's image.

Perhaps the difference between a saint and a sinner could
be expressed like this: a saint is a sinner who is at home with
God; a sinner is a saint who is not home, *yet*. Once we grasp
this difference and allow it to overshadow all our attitudes we
have the antidote for the deadly virtues. We can never again
be proud of our virtue. We can never again separate humanity into the categories of "we" and "they"—"the good guys
versus the bad guys."

Dr. Charles Allen tells of a railroad conductor who retired
after thirty years of service. At his retirement party, he told
the well-wishers, "I have spent over half of my life helping
people to get home." [1] Once we understand the real difference
between saints and sinners, we shall stop trying to be good and
proud of it, and start spending our lives trying to help people
to get home. "There are only two kinds of men: the righteous
who believe themselves sinners; the rest, sinners, who believe
themselves righteous." [2]

NOTES

INTRODUCTION

1. Dorothy Sayers, *Christian Letters to a Post-Christian World: Selected by Roderick Jellema* (Grand Rapids, Mich.: William B. Eerdmans Publishing Company, 1969), pp. 23–30.
2. Sayers, *Christian Letters*, p. xi.
3. Ibid., p. 23.
4. Ibid.
5. Reinhold Niebuhr, *Beyond Tragedy: Essays on the Christian Interpretation of History* (New York: Charles Scribner's Sons, 1937), p. 131.
6. Blaise Pascal, *Pensées*, trans. W. F. Trotter (New York: E. P. Dutton and Company, 1958), fragment 245, p. 85.

CHAPTER 1

1. Roger Shinn, *The Sermon on the Mount* (New York: Abingdon Press, 1962), p. 68.
2. Harry Emerson Fosdick, *Dear Mr. Brown* (New York: Harper and Row, 1961), p. 170.
3. Harry Emerson Fosdick, *The Living of These Days* (New York: Harper and Row, 1956), p. 35.
4. Lofton Hudson, *Grace Is Not a Blue-Eyed Blond* (Waco, Tex.: Word Books, 1968), p. 31.
5. Erich Fromm, *The Heart of Man* (New York: Harper and Row, 1964), pp. 39–42.
6. Sören Kierkegaard, "The Domestic Goose," *The Journals of Kierkegaard*, trans. Alexander Dru (New York: Harpers, 1958), pp. 252–53.
7. John 8:1–11.

CHAPTER 2

1. Nicholas Von Hoffman, "Mush God Competes Against Born-Agains," Austin (Tex.) *Daily Texan,* February 14, 1978, p. 4.
2. *Interpreter's Bible,* (New York: Abingdon Press, 1951), vol. 7, p. 326.
3. Carlisle Marney, Harvard Chapel address, 1972.

CHAPTER 3

1. Speech to the Christian Life Commission of the Southern Baptist Convention, October, 1972.

CHAPTER 4

1. Langdon Gilkey, *Shantung Compound* (New York: Harper and Row, 1966), p. 185.

CHAPTER 5

1. John 3:7.
2. Helmut Thielicke, *The Trouble With the Church,* trans. J. W. Doberstein (New York: Harper and Row, 1965), p. 3.
3. Ibid., p. 4.
4. Kierkegaard, *Journals,* p. 218.
5. For an excellent discussion of the underlying similarities between liberal and conservative interpreters of Scripture, see Bernard Ramm, *Special Revelation and the Word of God* (Grand Rapids, Mich.: Eerdmans, 1961), pp. 13–27.
6. Ibid., p. 174.

CHAPTER 6

1. Harry Emerson Fosdick, "Jesus' Ethical Message Confronts the World," in *Living Under Tension* (New York: Harper and Row, 1941), p. 166.
2. Ibid.

CHAPTER 7

1. Boris Pasternak, *Doctor Zhivago* (New York: Signet Publications, 1962), p. 39.
2. Harry Emerson Fosdick, *For The Living of These Days*, p. 272.
3. Ibid.
4. Ernest T. Campbell, "Religion A La Carte," *Sermons From Riverside* (New York: Riverside Church, October 18, 1970), p. 1.
5. Russell Bow, *The Integrity of Church Membership* (Waco, Tex.: Word Books, 1968), p. 34.
6. 1 Corinthians 12:12–36.
7. Paul Tournier, *Escape From Loneliness*, trans. John S. Gilmour (Philadelphia: Westminster Press, 1962), p. 60.
8. Mark 9:35.

AFTERTHOUGHT

1. Charles Allen, sermon delivered at the First Methodist Church, Houston, Texas, August, 1976.
2. Pascal, *Pensées*.